THE
HEART OF
INNOVATION

THE
HEART OF
INNOVATION

A Field Guide for Navigating to
Authentic Demand

Matt Chanoff, Merrick Furst,
Daniel Sabbah, and Mark Wegman

Berrett–Koehler Publishers, Inc.

Berrett-Koehler Publishers, Inc.
1333 Broadway, Suite 1000
Oakland, CA 94612-1921
Tel: (510) 817-2277
Fax: (510) 817-2278
www.bkconnection.com

ORDERING INFORMATION

Quantity sales. Special discounts are available on quantity purchases by corporations, associations, and others. For details, contact the "Special Sales Department" at the Berrett-Koehler address above.

Individual sales. Berrett-Koehler publications are available through most bookstores. They can also be ordered directly from Berrett-Koehler: Tel: (800) 929-2929; Fax: (802) 864-7626; www.bkconnection.com.

Orders for college textbook / course adoption use. Please contact Berrett-Koehler: Tel: (800) 929-2929; Fax: (802) 864-7626.

Distributed to the U.S. trade and internationally by Penguin Random House Publisher Services.

Berrett-Koehler and the BK logo are registered trademarks of Berrett-Koehler Publishers, Inc.

Printed in the United States of America

Berrett-Koehler books are printed on long-lasting acid-free paper. When it is available, we choose paper that has been manufactured by environmentally responsible processes. These may include using trees grown in sustainable forests, incorporating recycled paper, minimizing chlorine in bleaching, or recycling the energy produced at the paper mill.

Library of Congress Cataloging-in-Publication Data

Names: Chanoff, Matt, author. | Furst, Merrick, author. | Sabbah, Daniel, author. | Wegman, Mark, author.
Title: The heart of innovation : a field guide for navigating to authentic demand / Matt Chanoff, Merrick Furst, Daniel Sabbah, and Mark Wegman.
Description: First Edition. | Oakland, CA : Berrett-Koehler Publishers, [2023] | Includes bibliographical references and index.
Identifiers: LCCN 2023017217 (print) | LCCN 2023017218 (ebook) | ISBN 9781523005703 (paperback) | ISBN 9781523005710 (pdf) | ISBN 9781523005727 (epub) | ISBN 9781523005741 (audio)
Subjects: LCSH: New products | Branding (Marketing)
Classification: LCC HF5415.153 C424 2023 (print) | LCC HF5415.153 (ebook) | DDC 658.5/75—dc23/eng/20230508
LC record available at https://lccn.loc.gov/2023017217
LC ebook record available at https://lccn.loc.gov/2023017218

First Edition
31 30 29 28 27 26 25 24 23 10 9 8 7 6 5 4 3 2 1

Book producer: Susan Geraghty
Text designer: Cindy Butler
Cover designer: Adam Johnson

We dedicate this book to our families, for their inestimable support and tolerance and for the joy they bring us. To Lisa, April, Karen, and Dana; Yael, Talia, Eli, Jesse, and Nina; Jason, Anya, and Lovely; Emily, Zachary, and Mark; and Mackey and Marley.

CONTENTS

FOREWORD

Blockbusters dominate our perception of innovation. The Xerox machine. The IBM PC. Apple's iPhone. The Boeing 737. The Volkswagen Golf. But the path to innovation is more often defined by failure than by success, with around two-thirds of all market launches collapsing within a year. This leads to huge financial losses and millions of lost hours of engineering, design, and marketing work. The constraints on economic growth and development are clear and significant.

The Heart of Innovation tackles this urgent challenge with the novel approach of examining the demand side of innovation through the lens of a deeply layered understanding of human behavior. The result is a comprehensive guide to assessing "authentic demand" and a powerful new tool for innovators.

In the same way that the emerging study of human behavior fundamentally altered economic theory, we now have insights into how blind spots, biases, and false assumptions can impact innovation. *The Heart of Innovation* introduces valuable concepts anyone can use to avoid some of the thinking errors that commonly thwart the creation of new products.

Many of these thinking errors are well known: seeking out information that confirms our existing beliefs; continuing to invest time, money, and resources in a project because of what we've already put into it; misunderstanding information based on the way it is presented or framed. In a classic example, patients will consistently choose a doctor who describes a medical procedure as having a 90 percent success rate over another doctor who describes the same procedure as having a 10 percent failure rate.

There are plenty of famous cases of bias impacting business innovation. Because of its bias for the status quo, Kodak failed to embrace digital photography despite having invented the first digital camera. The same bias delayed Blockbuster's pivot to online streaming and subscription-based models. In the case of AOL, a false-consensus bias led to an assumption that its customers wanted a closed, proprietary platform.

Despite our human fallibilities, we're still rational creatures capable of producing life-altering innovations. We put a man on the moon, split the atom, turned sand into computer chips, and unlocked our own genetic code.

Innovation remains a powerful force, but it is not easy. Contrary to popular belief, innovation rarely relies on a "eureka moment." It is often a slow, grinding process. As this uniquely insightful book reveals, that process should start by developing a rigorous, science-based approach to identifying authentic demand and recognizing the effects of bias. Doing this is essential for innovation to thrive.

Whether you are an entrepreneur creating a consumer product, a business leader trying to come to grips with shifting markets and client behaviors, or simply a curious mind, *The Heart of Innovation* is an excellent innovator's guide for success.

Arvind Krishna
Chairman and CEO, IBM

INTRODUCTION

Frederick Buechner went right to the heart of why we wrote this book when he said, "The place God calls you to is the place where your deep gladness and the world's deep hunger meet."[1] This book has nothing to do with religion, and Buechner was talking about a spiritual calling, but being an innovator really does mean being called to where your deep gladness and the world's deep hunger meet.

This idea helps us understand the difference between innovation and invention. Yes, innovators can be inventors too; they can take pleasure in inventing beautiful things or constructing technological marvels. But the deepest gladness of innovators is to make and do things that make a difference. In the commercial world, that means making a difference to a market full of customers and clients. In the nonprofit and academic worlds, it means making a difference for beneficiaries and students. In all these areas, the innovation isn't complete if the hoped-for beneficiaries are indifferent—if the innovation doesn't, in one sense or another, sell.

On the surface, innovation looks like an exercise in self-actualization. Innovators are inspired with a solution to what they perceive as a problem or an opportunity. Sometimes the inspiration comes from thinking long and hard about the problem, which strikes a spark. Sometimes the inspiration comes from something narrower and more personal—a stroke of lightning, long experience, maybe undefinable creativity. Wherever inspiration comes from, the innovator is invested because the inspiration is a manifestation of their deep self. The motivation to drive it and see it through is a matter of pride, validation, and ambition.

That's part of the story. But a key part is missing, a small nuance that very often spells the difference between success and failure. Successful innovation also must connect with the deep selves, the motivations, the pride, validation, ambition, et cetera *of the people for whom the innovation is intended.* Not only the innovator's deep gladness, but also the world's great hunger.

Any good marketer might read that and think "of course, how obvious." Good marketers do their best to pay attention to their customers' hunger. They know that customers look for solutions. They know all about the framing and influencing factors that steer customers in one direction or another. But when it comes to innovation, marketers are usually too late. True innovations come at the very beginning of things. Marketers market what they're given, or on the basis of theories about the product they've been given. The same is true of most innovations that come out of innovation labs and design companies—they can be fabulous new solutions to known problems. But in those situations, the innovators too are also starting too late. They start with a prompt, an idea about a need or problem, and they go to work looking for new ways to address it. But by then, assumptions about needs and problems are baked into the project, viewed through the distorted lens of an invented solution. Too often, they find themselves marketing square pegs to round holes. Unexamined or improperly examined assumptions may still happen to be correct. But most often they're not. And when they're not, no amount of inventiveness or human-centered design or marketing can save them. Innovators can't reach authentic demand with a clever solution to the wrong problem, and marketers can't successfully market when the customers or clients are essentially indifferent.

This book centers around understanding and creating the conditions for authentic demand. Authentic demand isn't a matter of desire. It isn't the product of rational decision-making, or irrational influences from tricks of marketing or framing, or solutions to problems. Authentic demand is a different way of looking at the whole issue of demand.

Imagine a river. There's a small town on one side of the river and a factory on the other. The people who work at the factory live in the town. At 5:00 p.m., the factory whistle blows and the workers make their way home. Some go to the riverbank, where they've left little boats, and row their way home. Some walk upstream to where the river is shallow and ford their way across. A few people have invested in bigger boats, and they sell tickets to get across.

But then an innovator comes along, builds a bridge, and puts up a toll booth. Pretty soon, nearly all the factory workers get into the habit of paying the toll and walking across the bridge.

What demand looks like depends on where you sit. The bridge builder/toll taker sees overwhelming demand: every day, hordes of people head for the bridge and fill up the cash box at the toll booth. But from the customers' point of view, there's no intense desire, no clamoring for the product. The customers are not rationally solving problems. They're not irrationally being influenced by marketing. *Authentic demand is the demand of people who find themselves in a situation where buying and using a product or service is just a thing they do as part of living their lives.*

Before the innovation, the workers went about their business using the tools at hand—boats, the shallow ford upstream, or whatever. After the bridge went up they kept going about their business, only now the tool at hand is a bridge. The shift to using this new tool wasn't universal and automatic. But after the shift occurred, often after it was simply thought of, going back to the old way just wasn't on the menu. Using a boat would make you look and feel like an oddball. Fording, if you happen to even think about it, now seems dangerous or unpleasant. Of course there will be exceptions, but not using the bridge will seem like a violation of acting normally, an exception to the rule. That's what we mean by "not not" (which you will be reading about later): people will not *not* use the bridge.

That's authentic demand. But finding it is tricky. The situation we've described here—workers, factory, river, and so on—is incomplete and can easily mislead. Suppose those workers typically went fishing from their boats on the way home, and brought home fish for dinner. Suppose there was prestige attached to being in the river-fording club. Suppose someone was building a new housing development on the factory side. Any of those details, and thousands more, might mean that no one uses the bridge. This book describes a method and offers tools and rules of thumb to help innovators and people who work with them to understand the actual situations that markets of people find themselves in, in the necessary relevant detail, so that the products and services that innovators offer will fit into and become part of customer situations.

The four authors of this book have spent a good part of their lives inventing, innovating, and working alongside innovators as managers, investors, teachers, and CEOs. You'll see Danny's story, bringing IBM into the internet age, in chapter 5. Danny has had a forty-year career at IBM, starting and/or running divisions of the company with thousands of people working for him and billions of dollars at stake. He's now a consultant to IBM and to private equity firms and hedge funds. In chapter 8, you'll see Merrick and Matt's story of starting a company called Damballa. Merrick has founded eight startups, has been a tenured professor of computer science at Carnegie Mellon and Georgia Tech, and was head of the International Computer Science Institute at UC Berkeley. Merrick founded the Center for Deliberate Innovation at Georgia Tech and (together with Matt) Flashpoint@Georgia Tech, a business accelerator where many of the ideas in this book were developed. Besides collaborating with Merrick on Damballa, Flashpoint, a seed-stage venture fund, and other projects, Matt has been an angel investor in dozens of companies and sits on nonprofit boards around the world. Mark is a leading scientist and innovator at IBM, with over one hundred patents and papers in leading engineering journals, and more than seventeen thousand citations to his name. His inventions are behind many IBM innovations, and his wisdom with regard to recognizing and articulating the gap between invention and innovation appears throughout the book.

What drew Merrick and Matt to the work that led to writing this book was an authentic demand to help startup companies succeed, and to do it in a way that had intellectual depth and merit. Danny and Mark were drawn to the core of ideas, tools, and vocabulary we developed. The germ of the book began when Merrick and Matt started putting lessons they were learning while working with startups at Flashpoint into a series of blog posts. Our progress on putting the Flashpoint practice down on paper gained traction when Danny and Mark opened our eyes to challenges of innovation at the highest levels of corporate America. Mark's inventions at IBM are fundamental to every GIF format image and every optimizing compiler, but again and again he saw the company struggle to take advantage of his and his colleagues' breakthrough technologies. Danny's jobs at IBM have often centered around turning breakthroughs into products, so he saw many of the same problems from a management perspective. The ideas, language, and tools coming together at

Flashpoint struck both of them as directly applicable to situations they'd struggled with. This book encapsulates the lessons we've learned in four different areas where innovation matters: startups and small companies, large corporations, nonprofits, and universities. We wrote this book for innovators and for the people who help them out in all those places.

The book is divided into two parts. Part I, Accidental Innovation, chronicles successes and failures in innovation that have come about through innovators' finding, or failing to find, authentic demand. After we introduce the problem of indifference in chapter 1, chapter 2 describes a small rural company, Humminbird Fish Finder, and its leader, Jim Balkcom. Jim followed all the best procedures in deciding on their newest product—he talked to customers, got advice from experts, tested different versions, and so on. The company would have gone bankrupt doing all that, except for a chance conversation in a bait-and-tackle shop. Instead, the company became more successful than anyone involved ever dreamed. Chapter 3 introduces an even less likely success: an innovator who was one of the most powerless people on the planet, who changed her community with a simple "product": a scream.

Chapters 4 through 6 describe and analyze three distinct types of innovation, which we call informative, transformative, and formative. The cases in this section of the book include one of IBM's greatest successes, one of the company's most disappointing failures, SoulCycle, and a strip mall outside Philadelphia.

Part II, Deliberate Innovation, is devoted to the steps innovators ought to take to find and innovate around authentic demand deliberately. Chapter 7 describes Merrick and Matt's first steps toward a theory of authentic demand. Chapter 8 focuses on the biases, cognitive illusions, and blind spots that stand in the way of reaching it. Chapter 9 outlines how Merrick and Matt at Flashpoint, and Danny at IBM, worked to create cultures and innovation environments that helped tame these challenges. Chapters 10 and 11 describe the two central tools Merrick and Matt developed for uncovering unmet authentic demand—situation diagrams and Documented Primary Interactions (DPIs). More detailed instructions for conducting DPIs are in the appendix. More information about Deliberate Innovation is available at cdi.gatech.edu.

At heart, innovators are rebels. They commit themselves to doing something differently, to doing it their way. Deliberate Innovation doesn't take that away. Finding unmet authentic demand can't be reduced to a series of steps overseen by managers. The journey is always through an unknown landscape to a goal that's at best partly imagined. It requires courage, persistence, creativity, adaptability, and hard work—all the things that any adventure requires. Our hope and wish is that this book provides the tools for the journey.

PART ONE ←
ACCIDENTAL
INNOVATION

Authentic demand is the motivating force behind success in innovation. Part I dives into cases where innovations have succeeded and others where they've failed, on account of whether the innovator was able to identify an authentic demand (or not). In each case, though, finding authentic demand was an accident. The clues came from chance remarks, outsiders' insights, guessing and checking, explicit requests from customers, and so on. Good accidents can happen, but all too often they don't. Describing authentic demand in action through these cases is meant to give you a sense of what it is, how it operates, and how to identify it. Later, in part II, we'll propose a deliberate methodology for uncovering it.

CHAPTER 1
Getting Unstuck

Paul Simon was once interviewed on the Dick Cavett show talking about how he wrote "Bridge over Troubled Water." He described how the first idea came together, and said, "Then I was stuck." Cavett asked him, "What do you mean by stuck?" and Simon said, "Everywhere I went led me to where I didn't want to be, so I was stuck."[1]

This book is for entrepreneurs, investors, managers, social activists, and all kinds of innovators who would like the paths they are on to lead them somewhere they want to go. Some of us find ourselves paralyzed; we cannot figure out what to do next. But more commonly we are stuck the way Paul Simon was, because what we are doing, even when it may look productive, isn't leading us to where we want to be. Joe Reger was a founder in an early Flashpoint cohort. His company, Springbot, became one of the fastest-growing startups in the country. Joe recently looked back on the to-do list he'd created for himself as he began the company. Every item on the list, things like creating logos and securing meetings with important people in the business, were just the sort of activities that can feel productive but that were going to keep him stuck. Joe says that in retrospect, accomplishing them or not turned out to have nothing to do with leading the company to success. He kept moving, but he was stuck.

Running in directions that don't lead you to where you want to be isn't merely unproductive—it's counterproductive. It not only fails to take you where you want to go but also gives you an excuse to avoid the problems you really need to be addressing.

Paul Simon's goal was a complete song. An innovator's goal is a complete innovation. Innovations aren't complete until they become embedded in the world outside the innovator's head. So, unlike a complete song, a complete innovation depends on other people adopting it and bringing it into their lives in some way—being involved with it, whether involved means joining the team or investing or partnering or (most important) buying and using the products. A lot of what we talk about here involves companies and products, but innovation goes beyond business. Innovative nonprofits, movements, ideas, and artworks too stand or fall not on their own isolated merits but on one key question: Are the people they're intended for indifferent to them, or do those people in some way bring the innovation into their lives?

Most of the things modern people do are the result of earlier successful innovations. But that doesn't mean innovation is easy; it's extraordinarily hard. Not hard in the sense of requiring a lot of effort (though that's often needed too), but hard in the sense of not knowing what to do, of getting stuck.

The core of sustained innovation in business and other organizations is reciprocity. The innovator does something that leads other people to do something that enables the innovator to keep doing whatever they were doing. *Together, the two sets of behaviors support each other in a repeating cycle, and that's the mechanism of a complete innovation.* Very often the innovation is formed into a product, and the "other people" are a market full of customers. The customers pay for the product, allowing the innovator to keep making it. In noncommercial organizations, such as nonprofits or political movements, reciprocity might be expressed in other ways. This book, though, will focus primarily on business innovations, both for new startups and for large enterprises.

Being stuck, as an innovator, means being unable to get the reciprocal dynamic going. There are many kinds of sticking points. A lot of work has been done, and a lot of advice has been published, on four broad categories of these sticking points: technical, marketing and sales, financial, and leadership.

- **Technology.** Innovators often get stuck because they can't actually make and produce the product they have in mind, complete with the features, costs, and volume production they're shooting for.

- **Marketing and sales.** They often get stuck not knowing how to proceed with getting their product in front of their would-be customers and convincing them to buy.

- **Finance.** They often get stuck because they can't raise money or produce goods and sell them profitably.

- **Leadership.** Innovators often get stuck putting together the right team and creating the right culture and work environment to make it all happen.

Go into your local library or bookstore or search the right category at Amazon and you'll find lots of books to read on each of these subjects.

The premise of this book is that there's a fifth category, a kind of elephant in the room that is usually ignored or waved away or danced around. Facing the fact that you're stuck in this fifth category is a courageous act. It's very easy to duck thinking about it critically until it's too late. But getting unstuck in this category is the most important job of all, and doing it sheds important light on all the others.

The hidden category is usually called demand, but to distinguish it from random purchasing activity we'll call it *authentic demand*. The opposite of authentic demand is indifference. Authentic demand arises when would-be customers experience *not* buying as a problem, as something they can't be indifferent to, almost as a violation of something important.

The overwhelming number of business ideas, new products, and startup companies simply don't meet authentic demand. No reliable statistics are available because definitions of innovation and of failure vary so much. But anecdotally, Clay Christiansen, maybe the most respected of twentieth-century business professors, estimated failure rates at more than 90 percent. At least that percentage of startups fail, and the data shows that the leading reason for those failures is customer indifference. Nonprofits and activist movements also fail at similar rates. Yet these staggering failure rates go mostly unnoticed by the public. Everyone knows the names of big tech company winners—Google, Amazon, Facebook, and so on. For each one of them, scores of search engines, online marketplaces, and social media platforms have gone bankrupt, and few people remember their names.

Overcoming sticking points in technology, marketing and sales, finance, and leadership are essential. Some of the challenges in each of those categories are very tough. The challenge of uncovering and addressing unmet authentic demand is equally tough and at least as essential, but receives almost no direct attention.

Innovators often think in terms of "value proposition" or "solving customers' problems" or "product/market fit." But these things are actually just proxies for authentic demand. The hope is that if you create a thing of value, others will authentically demand it, or that if you solve other people's problems, they'll demand your solutions, or that if you make something that fits into people's lives, the product and the market will come together like a cosmic jigsaw puzzle.

None of these proxies really get at the nature of authentic demand, so they can easily lead innovators astray. Value propositions are based on the assumption that if people value something for themselves—that is, they want it—they'll buy it. But the world is full of things people want and don't buy. Think for a moment of all the things you might tell yourself you want but never buy. The famous saying "If you build a better mousetrap, they will come" is, sadly, rarely true.

In the same way, solving people's problems is no guarantee that they'll buy. People are often happy to talk about their problems. Entrepreneurs sometimes come to us and vividly recount how a prospective customer cornered them and talked passionately about his problems. In their minds, the conversation validated the features they were planning to include in their product, as a way to solve all those problems. Now if that product were to succeed in the market and we looked back at it in retrospect, we'd probably make sense out of the situation by recounting the customer's problems and describing how the product solved them. But just as likely, the product would fail. And in that case it would be equally easy to make sense of the failure, this time highlighting aspects of the product and the market that did not match up. Every situation includes huge amounts of data that can easily be collected into a pattern or narrative to rationalize the result. *Without an understanding of authentic demand, product/market fit is indistinguishable from prior hopes or post hoc rationalizations.*

Not every innovator is stuck when it comes to authentic demand. Some luck into it, some have seemingly unerring instincts, others manage to persist and grope their way to it. But many more are like Paul Simon—they're stuck in the sense that everywhere they go, everything they do, leads them to where they don't want to be.

The test is simple: Do you have more demand than you can meet? If you do, then your problems and challenges lie in other areas. If not, Deliberate Innovation can help you uncover authentic demand.

CHAPTER 2
Finding Authentic Demand by Accident

At a coffee shop near you, or on a Zoom call next door, there's a good chance you'll find people planning to start something innovative. In corporate offices and marketing departments at nearly every large company, people are conceiving, designing, building, and launching innovative new products and businesses. Activists are planning new ways to get voters activated. Nonprofits are trying new ways to solve problems. Innovation is everywhere.

And it's failing everywhere. Remember Microsoft's Bob? Coors' Rocky Mountain Sparkling Water? Arch, the McDonald's hamburger with the grown-up taste? Google Glass? Hot Wheels and Barbie computers? Those big, expensive flops are just the tip of the iceberg. Between 90 and 95 percent of all new product launches fail. New startup companies fail at a similar rate. According to venture capitalists, 70 percent of the startups they fund fail, and that's just the startups that get VC money to begin with. VCs fund fewer than one in a hundred of the proposals they consider, and most companies that seek VC funding but don't get it also fail.[1]

All this failure wastes rivers of money. And more important than the money, it wastes countless hours of hard work by creative, energetic people, not to mention their hopes and dreams.

The cause of all this innovation failure isn't a mystery. It's the customers. They just don't buy enough to earn back the cost of a product launch or to sustain a startup. An analysis by CB Insights of startup postmortems showed that the three biggest causes of startup failure that founders cite are (1) running out of money (38 percent), (2) market failure (35 percent), and (3) being outcompeted (20 percent).[2] You can discount running out of money as a reason for startup failure; it's a consequence, not a cause. And you can count being outcompeted as a type of market failure; it just means your product failed in the market, for whatever reason. Only 8 percent of founders blamed their failures on products not working correctly. This is common in some industries, such as pharmaceuticals, but rare overall. There are other failure paths too—founders clash and split up, people burn out, costs are higher than expected. But by far the number-one reason innovative products fail is that the customers don't buy them.

This is a puzzle. People don't make the effort to start companies unless they think the product will sell. Product launches by large companies go through extensive market testing and stage-gate processes designed to avoid wasting time and effort on ideas that won't fly. Modern startups rarely have the resources for that kind of thing, but they do their own equivalent customer discovery and validation through a lean startup process or something like it. Most innovative products launch with the approval of prospective customers. Many of these products get a big push from marketing, advertisements, sales incentives, and all the tricks of today's consumer economy. So why do most of them fail?

It's not because marketers and advertisers don't know their business. It's been sixty years since the marketing guru Ted Levitt published his famous manifesto, *Marketing Myopia*, which has come to be associated with his often-repeated line: "People don't want to buy a quarter-inch drill. They want a quarter-inch hole!"[3] Marketers are always relearning that lesson, and it's a key insight. But it isn't enough for innovators. Innovation has to happen before marketing can be effective. Levitt knew that customers wanted quarter-inch holes because fastening things with the help of drilled holes was an established, uncontroversial part of how people went about fastening things; it wasn't an innovative thing to do. The underlying authentic demand was no longer a secret. That's true in established businesses in general. But innovations happen before secrets like that are uncovered.

Jim Balkcom and Humminbird

To watch a true secret of innovation being uncovered, come to the small town of Eufaula, Alabama, and meet Jim Balkcom.[4]

The Humminbird Fish Finder company in Eufaula started in the conventional way—with a hard-working entrepreneur, a clever idea, and some technical know-how. Its product was an adaptation of a Heathkit do-it-yourself sonar device, repurposed as an underwater fish locator for recreational fishermen. This was something new; up until that point, only commercial fishing vessels could afford fish finders. There was clear demand, and soon the company had $1 million in annual revenue. The inventor and CEO, a motorcycle-driving maverick with the improbable name of Yank Dean, brought on a young Harvard Business School–educated banker named Jim Balkcom. Over several years, Dean and Balkcom built a more reliable product and a vibrant company culture. Step-by-step, they grew the company to $6 million in revenue. Then tragedy struck. Dean died of a sudden heart attack. Balkcom went to the investors and told them, "I'm not much, but I'm all you've got." He was hired as the new CEO.

Balkcom's goal was to dominate the segment, which he estimated to be about $50 million. His marketing team worked hard to develop a thorough understanding of the current market. They watched people fish, held focus groups, and consulted with customers, prize-winning anglers, distributors, and retailers to figure out exactly what they wanted and needed. Balkcom then worked with his engineers and launched a new-and-improved version based on the latest market feedback.

To no avail. Sales didn't budge.

So Jim went through the time and expense of talking to even more customers and listening to their ideas for new features, and he launched a second new version.

No change in sales.

The team tried again. And again. Humminbird brought out no less than nine new versions of the product, each one with better features for finding fish and/or more convenience. They tried a squelch knob to help see the fish more distinctly, technology that worked in shallower water, technology that worked while the boat was moving, a more portable version, a more waterproof version, and a version that recorded on a spooled tape.

Nothing. Sales were flat. It felt for all the world as though roughly $6 million in revenue was all they could get from the market no matter what they tried. But after all the expense of nine new product launches, the company was in precarious shape. Now it was do or die. The team tried one more time.

This time it was different. The new product broke all sales records. It actually had fewer functions than the nine previous iterations, but new customers suddenly came out of the woodwork, buying two or three for every boat. The company didn't just increase its share of the estimated $50 million market; it blew right past it. The new fish finder generated $75 million in sales during the first year, and revenue continued growing until at its peak Humminbird had $120 million in annual sales.

That tenth version didn't succeed because the engineers had finally gotten the feature mix right. It succeeded thanks to a paradigm shift, a whole new understanding of the customers, which, in turn, forced a complete redesign of the company. Jim had been stuck, but thanks to a painfully won, late-dawning realization, he became unstuck. He was able to create a new situation for his customers, one where Humminbird fish finders played a central role.

In this sort of situation, customer demand is like a whirlpool, a market of people demanding the product, pulling it toward themselves in such a way that the demand itself clarifies what's needed to satisfy it—what product features, what energy and ingenuity and resources. Jim hadn't hit on a combination of features that got traction: he'd hit on traction. From there, he was able to know what to do.

Jim describes the paradigm shift this way: "We thought we were in the business of catching fish. But no—we were in the business of catching fishermen." That sounds simple, but it was a well-hidden insight. The mission of Humminbird Fish Finder was to sell devices that found fish underwater. It sold products labeled "fish finders" to customers who went fishing on boats and used the devices to look for fish. Every signpost pointed to building a more effective fish finder. But all that was just camouflage. Once Jim saw through it, everything changed.

All the work Jim had done to understand his customers came into focus. One thing he'd learned is that his typical customer owned a $30,000 boat and was up to date on payments, but lived in a trailer and was often behind on the rent. That seemed lopsided, but his research showed that they weren't fishing to eat; they were truly recreational fishermen. Taking their families out on the boat on weekends was their dearly bought escape, the part of their week that helped them get through the rest of it. Jim's attention shifted from the question of how to help these people catch fish to how to help them be recreational fishermen.

This is how it happened: Jim's VP of marketing, Tom Dyer, hired a marketing expert named Sue Symon. One day Sue approached a harried-looking woman at the fish finder shelf at a Bass Pro Shop and asked what she was buying.

"I don't care," said the woman. "My husband takes me and the kids out on the boat on weekends and it's as boring as hell. The kids go crazy. I thought maybe one of these would at least keep them entertained."

If it had been Tom or Jim or his engineers, with all their expertise in the technology of finding fish, they may have thought that this was a useless conversation. But it clicked in Sue Symon's head. The customers weren't only the fishermen. A lot of them were spouses. And the users weren't only fishermen; they were spouses and children who were stuck for long hours on a small boat every weekend, bored to tears while the guy fished. Sue recognized that there's more to a successful weekend fishing excursion than catching fish. She went back to Jim and told him that he was in the entertainment business.

Sue began using focus groups to confirm and explore the implications of this pivotal insight, bringing in women for the first time. Immediately, she started learning things that hadn't become apparent in her previous conversations with customers. The fish finder screens weren't usable in sunlight. The buttons and knobs were too complicated. The fish finders weren't sold where these customers shopped.

The revised understanding of the market that came out of these sessions got Jim and his company unstuck. It gave them a place to put all their energy and ingenuity and resources.

It allowed them to navigate the question of what features to offer. An entertainment device must be attractive to play with, not intimidating like a scientific instrument. Jim removed every button, knob, and gauge he could do without. He got a lot of pushback from his engineering department, who valued the technology they'd created and were resistant to the idea of change. But with a clearer vision of the customers, Jim was able to confidently overrule them. The finished product was the simplest fish finder on the market; even children stuck on a small boat could use it.

One feature that he decided was important to the entertainment market was a good screen. The fish finder screen was a spinning disk like that on a radar screen in a World War II movie. It was barely readable in sunlight. Jim went to his engineer Al Nunley and said, "Go around the world and don't come home until you find a display that works." Al went home and packed his bags. In Tokyo, at Hitachi, he found what they were looking for. LCD screens were brand new. The only ones on the market at that time were tiny screens on wristwatches. Jim and Al convinced the giant conglomerate to beta-test this new technology with their tiny fish finder company in Alabama. Humminbird became the first company in the world to commercialize modern LCD screens.

The insight into who the customers actually were also proved crucial for navigating sales and distribution. Fish finders were typically sold to distributors that serviced boat dealerships and sporting goods stores. But entertainment customers didn't frequent those places; they went to Walmart or shopped from the Bass Pro Shop catalog, neither of which depended on distributors. But choosing to sell directly was a big risk for Humminbird; the distributors saw Walmart as a threat and issued an ultimatum: if you sell through Walmart, you can't sell through us. Choosing the big-box store meant burning bridges. It would be nearly impossible to go back. Jim did it anyway.

Knowing the market also led Jim to build a new company culture. To sell electronic entertainment devices, Humminbird had to become a consumer electronics company. This was no small challenge for a company tucked into a rural town in south-central Alabama. It meant attracting, hiring, and retaining consumer electronics designers and engineers to the kind of town that that sort of person rarely heard about, let alone settled down in. The attention Jim had already paid to building a strong company culture paid dividends here, and he doubled down on building a company environment that could attract and retain the people he needed. Just to mention a few highlights: He convinced his partners to go along with putting 20 percent of the company's stock into an employee stock ownership plan (ESOP); he provided generous health insurance and worked to keep costs down by running company-wide "stop smoking" challenges and other fitness challenges; he stalked the factory floor offering $20 bills for correct answers to trivia questions. Twice, when the company hit sales milestones, his marketing director, Tom Dyer, filled a garbage bag with $100 bills and handed one out to every employee as they walked out the door, saying, "Have a nice weekend; see you Monday morning."

One simple but profound revelation gave Jim and Humminbird's other managers clear direction about what they needed to do moving forward to shape the product, the distribution channels, and key aspects of the company culture—virtually everything about the business. In short, Jim's new understanding of what business he was in allowed him to get unstuck.

In the end, understanding the market correctly made the company a huge success. It led to a $7 million payout on the company's ESOP. By then Jim had hundreds of employees, evenly divided between Black and white, including many who had lived in deep rural poverty without even running water in their homes. When the ESOP paid out, Balkcom stood on the shop floor handing out checks. People bought houses and cars with those checks, put children through college, and funded comfortable retirements. Jim found a true market, and the result was life changing, not only for him but for a whole community.

The Not Not Principle

Jim's breakthrough happened by accident. But by analyzing it properly we can start to see how to work toward such breakthroughs purposefully and methodically. Let's start by unpacking the story Sue Symon first heard.

Suppose you were that weekend angler heading out to fish with your family. What's that excursion about? What could happen that would ruin your day?

Here are three (out of many) possibilities:

1. Your boat springs a leak.

2. Your kids spend the whole time yelling, complaining, and carrying on.

3. You don't catch the maximum possible
   number of fish.

Among those possibilities, only the first two really matter to you. If either of them happens, it will ruin your day—maybe your whole week. But the third possibility ... really, who cares? If you need more fish, you can always pick them up at the supermarket.

Given these circumstances, are you likely to check that the boat won't leak? Do something to keep the kids entertained? How about buying something that helps you catch the maximum number of fish?

It's a complicated world, and people are never 100 percent predictable. No innovator or business leader could ever be in a position to confidently say, "My customer will definitely check that the boat doesn't leak or will definitely buy something to prevent their kids from complaining on the boat." But given these circumstances, it would be unlike a recreational angler to not check the boat; it would be unlike a recreational angler with kids on the boat to ignore them. Allowing the boat to sink or allowing the kids to scream would not be normal behavior; it would be a violation of normal behavior. These people, in this situation, can be counted on to act, for the most part, in a certain way. By contrast, it's perfectly common and normal for a recreational angler to finish the day without having caught the maximum possible number of fish. So there's no reason to believe that they'll buy some device to make that happen.

Put simply, the person in this circumstance will not *not* take care of the boat and not *not* see to the kids. These things won't happen every time, but they'll happen.

The world is full of situations that can be better understood by seeing the not nots. People will not *not* pinch their fingers in closing doors. Certainly fingers end up getting pinched, but you can rely on people to move their hands to avoid it happening. People will not *not* go to bed without having eaten. They will not *not* greet a friend they pass on the street. Parents will not *not* see that their children get home after school. Not nots are not musts. Sometimes they fail; sometimes people forget or circumstances intervene or more compelling not nots take precedence. But in any case, they matter. Also, not nots don't only show up in desperate situations. You can't place them somewhere on an intensity spectrum between whims and necessities. Also, they can't be categorized as conscious or unconscious. People don't walk around with a strong desire to avoid getting their fingers pinched in a door. They avoid it happening without intensity or conscious attention for the most part, but sometimes they're mindful and alert about it. To use the not not rule of thumb it isn't necessary to categorize something as important or not, or to worry about whether people are acting consciously or unconsciously.

Not nots are often hard to notice, because people typically just take care of them in the normal course of their days. Sometimes, though, they're noticeable in the adaptations people make to new circumstances. To take the example of parents seeing that their kids get home from school, it's possible to watch them adapting to situations that challenge the not not behavior. If the school bus isn't running that day, a parent will leave work to pick the kid up. If they can't leave work, they'll call a friend to do it, or text the child that they have to walk home that day, or call the school and demand that the child is safely taken care of until they can arrive. The world is always throwing us into new situations, and we generally cope, adapting to the situation so as to keep fulfilling our not nots.

Except when we can't. Sometimes situations change in such a way that people can't find an adaptation that works. Sometimes the ways we cope with one situation come into conflict with how we cope with another. In these circumstances, a product that offers people a new adaptation, so that they can keep fulfilling their not nots, will fly off the shelves.

The not not principle is useful not just for seeing new opportunities but for clarifying what to do once you've found them. Once Jim Balkcom identified his new not not, he could see that some features, such as an easily visible screen, met the demands of a not not. A person in the circumstance of using a fish finder as entertainment on a boat, watching what's going on underwater, would normally, typically, watch the screen. If they didn't, it would be weird. Therefore the device wouldn't play its role properly without a screen that was visible in bright sunlight. Other features that Jim had tried in his earlier iterations of the device—making it more portable or capable of recording or improving the squelch circuitry—didn't have that sort of quality. They weren't meaningful to customers in respect to the not not. Figuring out the details of

31

the features for the new device became a process of clarifying the details of a customer's circumstance and applying the not not rule.

The rule is useful not only in designing the product but in designing the company. As a company selling electronic entertainment devices to people who shop largely at Walmart, Humminbird Fish Finder could not *not* sell through Walmart. That meant it could not *not* jump through the inventory management and other hoops that Walmart demands of its suppliers.

Jim Balkcom didn't hear of the not not rule until long after he'd sold Humminbird Fish Finder. He felt his way, step by painful step, after coming to the insight that he was selling entertainment devices. But years later, when he happened to visit Flashpoint, it hit him with a powerful shock of recognition. Understanding the customer situation, and the business situation, in terms of not nots was exactly what he'd been up to.

For Jim and his colleagues at Humminbird, uncovering authentic demand was a matter of luck. It took open-mindedness and courage to see things differently and to act on that recognition. But they probably would never have gotten there on their own. Most likely, they would have continued iterating on fish finders that incrementally improved on the job of catching fish, without making a difference for the company. The not not for Humminbird was hidden in a blind spot, a kind of blind spot that isn't limited to small companies like Humminbird but plagues every enterprise from the smallest startup to the Fortune 500.

CHAPTER 3
Three Types of Innovation:
Informative, Transformative, and Formative

When innovations are successful, they're no longer innovative: they turn into unremarkable elements of a new equilibrium. Successful innovations are expressed as new sets of behaviors from all the stakeholders—behaviors that reinforce and sustain each other. Humminbird's successful innovation changed the behaviors of customers, people with jobs at Humminbird, other stakeholders such as distributors and suppliers, and potential stakeholders such as prospective customers and job applicants. As we'll see in a minute, the most impressive, Nobel Prize–winning technology innovations can fail to change behavior, while some innovations can establish a dramatic new equilibrium without any technology at all, without even a product. Let's start with Jane Achieng's innovation, which shows the process stripped down to its most basic elements.

Cultural Innovation in Microcosm: Jane the Innovator

Jane lives comfortably now, but in the 1990s she was a young mother living in something like hell. Kibera is one of the largest slums in the world. It's a sprawl of about eight hundred thousand people, squeezed improbably into the center of bustling Nairobi, Kenya, between nice neighborhoods full of beautiful homes with electricity, running water, sewers, paved roads, fire brigades, garbage pickup, and police. Kibera doesn't have any of that. It's an "unincorporated area," meaning that most city services stop at the border.

A lot of people call Kennedy Odede the mayor of Kibera. He's a superstar in the nonprofit world. He runs a 2.5 million-member network of poor people all over Kenya that not only provides desperately needed services but helps people move toward self-reliance and self-respect. Kennedy grew up, frequently homeless and starving, in the mud alleyways of Kibera.

Matt sat down with Kennedy to hear about some of his innovations. Matt's day job was as a startup investor and partner with Merrick at Flashpoint. He was also on Kennedy's board, and was interested in innovation in the nonprofit world as well as in startup companies. Instead of talking about the organization, Kennedy started talking about his mother, Jane Achieng.[1]

Picture a warren of long sheds connected by garbage-covered dirt roads. Each shed is made out of corrugated steel sheets, subdivided into a dozen ten-by-ten-foot rooms. At least five people, sometimes as many as fifteen, live in each of those rooms, each one opening onto the alley or a sewage ditch. Most rooms have a cot for the parents, a rug and maybe some blankets where the kids sleep, a corner with plastic bowls and dishes serving for a kitchen, and another corner with some shelves. That's home. Outside you can cook on a pile of charcoal, walk a few hundred meters and stand in line with a big yellow jerrycan to buy some water, toss your garbage or burn it, and find a place to defecate. Better not walk inside with those shoes, because they're pretty disgusting. But they'll be stolen if you leave them outside. Infant and child mortality is among the highest in the world. Welcome to Kibera.

But none of that was Jane's problem; that was just her neighborhood. Jane's problem was that her husband beat her. She wasn't the only one with this problem. Many of her friends had husbands who got drunk on *changaa*, the local home brew, and beat them. Even though being beaten was common, it was considered a disgrace, so women hid it. They tried not to cry out; they covered their bruises. They didn't discuss it.

One day, though, Jane had had enough. Talking with a bunch of her friends, she proposed something new. "If your husband hits you," she said, "don't keep quiet. Yell. Scream as loudly as you can. And if you hear one of us yelling, you start yelling too." They tried it. When one woman was beaten, instead of remaining silent she started to scream. Women in other homes heard the noise and started yelling. In a few minutes the whole neighborhood was in an uproar. And before long there were men pounding on the door of the one who was beating his wife, telling him to cut it out. He did, and the women tried it again next time. Jane's method became a custom, and in that neighborhood of Kibera the incidence of men beating their wives went down. No consciousness raising, no pepper spray or self-defense classes, no police intervention or emergency blue light boxes. Just an idea.

Telling the story today, Jane (now in her sixties) just says that the men found it annoying. But what seems to have happened is that Jane and her friends flipped the script. Before her radical innovation, it was disgraceful to be beaten; it was a symbol of wifely failure. Afterward, it was disgraceful to be a wife beater. The yelling, and the affirmation of others who joined in, introduced a new element into the situation. The underlying commitment to avoiding public shame remained constant, but the shame shifted to the abusers. The physical and demographic characteristics of Kibera were another constant: people crowded together in metal rooms where they could hear each other, domestic violence common enough that a chain reaction was possible. With the introduction of this one new idea, women began coping with their situations differently, and so did men.

As a new equilibrium got established, the innovation itself started fading out. Fewer men beat their wives, so the community screaming also became less frequent. But elements of the new equilibrium remained.

Twenty-five years later, in 2017, Kennedy had grown into the so-called mayor, and among other things he'd built a school in Kibera, the nicest, most modern building in the slum, with computers and science labs and everything needed for a good education. That was an election year, and when the election was disputed, riots and looting broke out. As usual, Kibera was the epicenter, and the school, with all its expensive equipment, made a tempting target for looters. One night some women heard their husbands planning a raid on the school.

When the men showed up the next day, they found a line of women protecting the school. There was shouting on both sides, but the men eventually went back home. They could physically have beaten those women down and broken into the school, carrying off computers that were worth a year's salary. But they didn't. Jane's innovation from twenty-five years earlier was all but forgotten by then. As far as anyone knows, there hasn't been a "community scream" in years. But some part of the change in behavior catalyzed by that innovation apparently lives on.

Cultural Innovation Writ Large

The number of people impacted by Jane Achieng's innovation was small, compared to the number of people whose behavior is impacted by IBM. About 280,000 people work for IBM. They, and millions of customers, suppliers, distributors, investors, and so on behave in reciprocal ways that sustain each other and sum up to sustaining the company as an entity. All that behavior is the expression of a corporate culture.

Corporate culture involves the values, beliefs, expectations, and incentives that determine how employees and management behave and interact, both among themselves and with their customers, suppliers, distributors, investors, and others. Of course the physical, human, and financial aspects of an organization also play into its culture. Since the 1960s, a lot of research has gone into understanding corporate cultures, dividing them into types and figuring out ways to improve them. There's been less attention paid to innovation itself, to dividing that into different types and to figuring out how corporate cultures engage differently with the different types of innovation.

All cultures include and exclude. Some activities and behaviors are within bounds, and some are out of bounds. Innovation risks going out of bounds, doing things that are not OK in a particular culture, and suffering the consequences. So management techniques that aim at fostering innovation tend to focus on incentivizing and making it safe for people to try new things. For example, in the 1980s, when Japanese companies appeared to be outcompeting and out-innovating American ones, William Ouchi's influential *Theory Z* included an argument that because Japanese employees were guaranteed a job for life, they could be more innovative—taking the time to try or learn new things didn't threaten their jobs.

There's nothing wrong with encouraging innovation or making it safer to innovate. But these approaches don't go far enough, because a lack of encouragement or feelings of insecurity are not the only obstacles to innovation. All the little rules and guidelines of culture do more than shape how people act; they shape how people think. Part of the culture of Humminbird was that the company satisfied customers by helping them catch fish. You couldn't get Jim and his colleagues to think in terms of helping them in a different way just by incentivizing or making it safe to be innovative. The idea of fish finders as recreational devices was in a blind spot where they just couldn't see it.

By definition, a blind spot can't be seen. But you can start to make sense of where blind spots tend to live, and one way to start doing that is paying attention to the difference between innovation and invention.

An *innovation* always involves a change in behavior. It's a sustainable, repeatable change that results in a new equilibrium, a change in the form of the culture itself. Innovations and inventions are distinct. An *invention* might be a flash in the pan, a new thing that's relegated to a research paper, incorporated into a product that doesn't sell and just doesn't change behavior. But sometimes inventions underlie innovations, which do change the form.

All innovations change an equilibrium situation that's being held in place by a culture. That can happen in three different ways, three different sorts of sustained changes in the form. We call them *informative*, **transformative**, and *formative*. *Informative* innovations are the ones that allow more of the same. They don't change the outward shape or total form. Instead, they fill up the form with new assets, enabling an established company to keep up with technological advancements or with competitors, and support incremental change to incrementally improve revenue or profit. Most R&D is directed toward informative innovation. *Transformative* innovations are the ones that change the form itself. They expand the range. Adaptive leadership is a management field focused on dealing with transformative innovation. *Formative* innovation is the least familiar and a particular focus for Deliberate Innovation.

Informative. These innovations improve something for customers or companies without changing the situation they're in. It's called informative because the form of the situation remains the same and the innovation happens inside that form, without changing the basic structure. Informative innovation leads to incremental improvements in products and gradual improvements in customers' lives, along recognized, established lines. An example of informative innovation is a railroad company that considers improving service by buying newer diesel engines or refrigerator cars.

Transformative. These innovations change the assumptions at the root of how customers or companies behave in a situation. Questioning assumptions can lead to reshaping how companies or customers think of their environment or situation. It is called transformative because it changes the form of the situation. Transformative innovation can lead to a quantum leap in opportunities. One example might be a railroad company that reimagines itself as a transportation company, leveraging its in-house expertise in logistics and customer relationships to address opportunities in shipping or air freight.

Formative. Formative innovations are the ones that led to forming the situation in the first place. Virtually every successful company starts by forming something new, something that isn't incremental and isn't a transformation of something else. One example is the formation, in the 1890s, of Herman Hollerith's Computing-Tabulating-Recording Company (CTR). CTR innovated a new form: management of large-scale data. The company's name was later changed to IBM.

Understanding the differences between the three types of innovation helps with expanding opportunities and guarding against challenges. Each type of innovation has its own problems and its own most effective tools. Often a leader who's good at one type of innovation is less effective at another. Innovators in large companies regularly fail to meet challenges because they limit themselves to informative mindsets and tools, or because they underestimate the challenges of transformative innovation, or because they underestimate the worth of formative innovation (which starts small).

Paying attention to one type of innovation and not noticing the others is a type of blind spot. To see more clearly, innovators can ask themselves, "What type of innovation might make sense here?" or remind themselves, "When I'm stuck, it might be because I'm thinking about the wrong kind of innovation." *Deliberate Innovation involves considering and choosing a type of innovation to focus on, understanding the challenges that come with the territory, and using the right tools for the job.*

CHAPTER 4
Informative Innovation: GMR

Most innovation, measured by time and money spent, is informative—and that's how it should be. It's the type of innovation that's synonymous with improvement. It's the primary way that companies keep up with or beat competitors, leverage new technologies, and put creative minds to work. It's usually where businesses engage in deep science and engineering, and where careers can be cultivated. Successful companies don't slack off on informative innovation, because in a dynamic economy, standing still is losing—losing initiative, losing a share of the customer's wallet, and losing share value.

Sometimes, though, seeking improvement isn't the right approach. Sometimes an innovator is better off shifting their understanding of a problem or opportunity (transformative). Sometimes they're better off uncovering and addressing entirely new problems and opportunities (formative).

GMR and WebSphere, two examples from IBM's history, illustrate the dangers and challenges of choosing the wrong kind of innovation and the opportunities that open up when you choose the right one. GMR was an invention that IBM implemented as an informative innovation. A rival properly recognized it as a transformative opportunity for consumers, and IBM's business suffered. WebSphere was an innovation (not particularly based on an invention at all) that one of us (Danny) recognized and helped implement as transformative. (We tell the WebSphere story in chapter 5.)

In 1997, scientists at IBM made a breakthrough. They took a recent scientific discovery, called giant magnetoresistance, and used it to build a new kind of hard disk. Giant magnetoresistive heads for hard disks (GMRs) were expected to revolutionize the hard disk industry. Hard disk size and cost were closely related to a metric called areal density—the amount of data that could be stored on a given area of the disk. With its patented GMR technology, IBM could store more data on the same-size disk, or make smaller disks that held the same data as their competitors' large ones.

IBM scientists and marketers were proud of their achievement. Figure 4.1 shows a press release from the period.

It's an understatement to say that IBM management was excited about this technology. They thought it was revolutionary, and had plausible reasons for that view. They thought that GMR blew competitors like EMC out of the water. They knew their customers well; they'd heard loud and clear that disk space was a huge problem that could only get worse. With superior technology, IBM had leapfrogged the competition. Leaders at the company imagined a future with computers everywhere, and tiny

IBM disk drives embedded in everything from cars to toasters. Despite being some of the smartest and most creative materials scientists of the era, they made the mistake of imagining the use of the technology through a limited, informative lens.

They weren't alone. Others were also innovating in the space and were also looking at their technical achievements through an informative lens. While IBM was developing GMR as a technology for higher-capacity disk drives, David Patterson at UC Berkeley and his colleagues had come up with a way of linking cheap hard disks together, based on a system called RAID (redundant arrays of inexpensive disks). While the people at IBM were laser-focused on increasing areal density, thinking that was the key to the storage market, Patterson and his colleagues were

---

The Giant Magnetoresistive Head: A Giant Leap for IBM Research

It's called the Giant Magnetoresistive effect. Ten years ago, it hadn't even been discovered. But now, after intense and dedicated research and development, "giant magnetoresistance"—or GMR for short—makes its mass-market debut in IBM's record-breaking 16.8-gigabyte hard disk drive for desktop computers using a special GMR structure developed at IBM called a spin valve.

Most people don't give their hard drive a second thought—until they run out of disk space. If this describes you, read on. Once you understand the beauty of the GMR/spin valve head, you will never feel the same way about your hard disk drive again.

Figure 4.1. GMR press release

Source: Frank Hayes, "The Story So Far," reprinted in *Computerworld*, November 17, 2003.[1]

focused on something else: speeding up access to data. When information is scattered around a single disk, the head picks up a bit of data from a particular spot on the disk and then may have to wait until the disk spins around again to get the next bit. The disks spin quickly, but in the game of accessing data, milliseconds matter. Patterson thought that by distributing the data onto two disks that were both spinning, you could cut the time till the next bit was read, and speed things up. Like his competitors at IBM, Patterson had a fixed assumption. Their assumptions differed in detail—capacity versus speed—but they both amounted to a common view that faster, higher-capacity disks were what the market demanded. These assumptions were completely reasonable. Customers, industry journals, and scientists all talked about digital storage in terms of speed and capacity. Customers assessed products in those terms, and competitors competed on those metrics.

But when Patterson demonstrated his RAID technology for potential collaborators and tech reporters, something unexpected happened. The purpose of the demo was to show off the speed of his new RAID system. Almost as an afterthought, at the end of the demo, he dramatically pulled one of the hard disks out of the RAID system. Because the same data was on each disk, the system kept working, just a bit slower. To his surprise, it was that afterthought that caught the attention of the market.

In an interview a few years later, Patterson recalled:

> We were still performance-oriented, thinking RAID was for performance, so we were shocked to see

somebody write this up in *Byte* magazine. The PC community was obviously not so performance-oriented as it was dependability-oriented, and they thought, 'Hey, less-expensive dependable computing.' . . . It really just took off after that. EMC decided to build mainframe storage out of PC disks.

So EMC took the lead and RAID systems made it into computers, largely on the basis of dependability. To Patterson's surprise, the performance issue didn't drive the market, and to IBM's surprise, miniaturization wasn't a key advantage either. Instead, reliable, dependable, easy-to-manage RAID systems took off, eventually evolving toward server farms and creating the infrastructure behind social platforms, streaming videos, and the modern web.[2]

The article in *Byte* magazine played the same role in the world of hard disks that Sue Symon's insight about fish finders as entertainment devices played for Humminbird. Like Jim Balkcom, EMC heard the message. IBM didn't.

Authentic demand for reliability was hiding in plain sight. Everyone in the market knew it was important—of course hard disks had to work. The critical metric was "mean time between failures" (MTBF). Acceptable MTBF standards were well known and available, and all the new disk drives from IBM, EMC, and other competitors met them. In hindsight, though, it's clear that if the MTBF is steady while the disk capacity goes up, there's trouble ahead. If a drive holding sixteen gigs of important company information fails, the company will have a bigger problem than if a one-gig disk were to fail. For the overall risk to remain the same, the MTBF standards would have to increase in step with disk capacity. No one in the market was paying attention to that—until the fateful moment when David Patterson yanked a live hard disk out of a RAID system.

It wasn't that the people at IBM just happened to be looking the other way at that moment and failed to recognize the authentic demand; that mistake was a long time coming. Patterson could casually pull a hard disk out of a RAID system thanks to his pioneering work on software for managing hard disks. Ironically, there was a team at IBM that had done a lot of similar work, and even owned some important patents in the area. But that was software. IBM was a hardware company where software only played a supporting role. The groups at IBM responsible for moving research to development to market were hardware groups. They didn't recognize what they had.

The philosopher Schopenhauer died before IBM was even founded, but he anticipated the fate of GMR when he wrote, "Just as a stream flows smoothly on as long as it encounters no obstruction, so the nature of man and animal is such that we never really notice or become conscious of what is agreeable to our will; if we are to notice something, our will has to have been thwarted, has to have experienced a shock of some kind."[3] The shock IBM leaders experienced was the shock of watching EMC capture the hard disk business right out from under their revolutionary technical achievement with GMR. They'd been on the right track imagining a future with computer systems showing up in every sort of consumer product, even toasters. But the path to that future, at least the path that led to revenue and profit, didn't run through IBM.

GMR was a blockbuster invention from a scientific and technological point of view. But for all the talk of a revolutionary new technology, the people at IBM were only able to think of the market in nonrevolutionary, informative terms. Reasoning that goes from the invention to the market is more subject to cognitive biases and illusions than going the other way—from thinking first about the market. The inventions themselves—GMR and RAID—weren't what mattered; what mattered was the market's authentic demand.

Challenges to Informative Innovation

Every type of innovation has its particular challenges, which can best be met with tools that are specific to the job. The challenges that face incremental, informative innovation are the best known and best managed. That's not to say that overcoming these challenges is easy or unimportant. These are the innovations necessary to maintain and improve the revenue, market share, and margins that are the core of an established business. Work on this sort of innovation properly consumes the bulk of the R&D budgets of most companies. Accordingly, most of the literally thousands of books on innovation focus on improving (informative) innovation cultures. Techniques include the following:

- Rewarding employees for innovation or reducing their risks

- Encouraging factory-floor employees to share ideas

- Supporting broad opportunities for employee education

- Making time and bringing in consultants to provide design thinking sessions and similar programs

- Employing open-plan office design, group activities, and other techniques for bringing together people from different sides of a company to cross-fertilize ideas

- Implementing accessible processes for innovation ranging from stage-gate procedures to contests to field trips

These techniques are examples of the many ways companies increase or improve informative innovation. But these sorts of programs do not address the two major limitations that are inherent in informative innovation itself: *maturity* and *sustainability*.

Maturity. Informative innovation tends to lead to mature industries and technologies that naturally yield fewer advances as time goes on. This is the famous "S-curve" discussed in MBA programs. The curve is used to illustrate that at some point markets become more saturated, competition kicks in, and the benefits to customers of each new feature or technological improvement decrease. Incrementalism reaches an inflection point where an S-curve of growth tends to flatten out.

Sustainability. A career in leading businesses and sales forces taught Danny to keep one eye on sales and the other eye on business sustainability. Thinking about sales and making transactions happen are necessary in the short term, but they don't address the issue of long-term sustainability. Markets aren't static, and new technologies, demographics, competitors, regulations, and public moods can undermine the assumptions that sustain any business. When managers focus exclusively on current sales targets and other metrics, they easily lose sight of trends and technical developments that threaten to leave whole families of products and services behind. Keeping an eye on informative innovation as a whole, in the context of different types of innovation, provides an essential guardrail for any mature business.

The GMR technology eventually found its way into most hard drives, but never reaped the benefits expected. Where GMR failed, WebSphere—IBM's entry into enabling web-based transactions for e-commerce—succeeded. The success wasn't based on a technical innovation but on an innovation in mindset, a different way of seeing things.

CHAPTER 5
Transformative Innovation: WebSphere

Hurricane Floyd was raging up and down the East Coast. Just before it came ashore, Danny had flown to an IBM facility in North Carolina to meet a different kind of storm. Danny was a vice president at IBM, and one of his key responsibilities was getting its internet business off the ground. Inside the building, an auditorium full of people was watching an argument unfold. The director of one of IBM's largest software labs stood up and raised his voice. He was making a technical argument, describing why his approach to launching IBM into the web business was the right one. But it was technical only on the surface. Danny listened and responded. When the yelling started, Danny just kept nodding. Finally, the diatribe ended with "I don't care what you think. It's my lab and we're going to do it my way."

Danny nodded again. Later that week he made sure that the lab's budget was significantly reduced. It was going to be done Danny's way.

Before the advent of the web, the only people who interacted with a company's IT systems were employees. Today, literally billions of people routinely interact directly with computer systems to shop, do their banking, and for a thousand other reasons, all without a company employee in the middle. IBM played a central role in that transition for many enterprises across the globe. Over a ten-year period, IBM developed an $8 billion annual business for direct interaction. All built on the back of the WebSphere brand.

The GMR story shows that inventions, even great ones, don't show the way to innovation by themselves. The WebSphere story shows how great innovations don't have to come from new inventions at all.

In the late 1980s, IBM was facing competition on many sides, losing market share and looking toward a bleak future. On the software side, the company still made the core databases and tools that most large enterprises used to store and manage their data and transactions. But the ground had shifted, leading to a tangle of new opportunities and challenges:

- For decades, the core of what IBM did for customers was help them store and update information. In this new environment, customers still needed to store and update data, but now they also needed to distribute it around the world, provide access directly to customers on the fly, provide their customers with interactivity, and at the same time record and control the interactions. Other companies were taking the lead in meeting these emerging needs.

- The rise of personal computing added more competition to the market and also raised customer expectations of how easily they could use software.

- IBM's tools had to work with a flood of automation tools that were coming from IBM's competitors and from startups.

- There was a whole new community of stakeholders. For IBM to be part of the internet revolution, these new stakeholders, particularly developers who were using standards such as Microsoft's Windows and Sun Microsystem's Java, had to buy in to IBM's products and ecosystem.

IBM was used to being the world's hub for enterprise-level hardware and software solutions, but it was losing market share, and Microsoft was gaining. Microsoft led with new architectures and tools for enterprises based on PCs and cheaper servers connected with local area networks (LANs). With a LAN, some operations and data remained on a user's PC, but most stayed on a remote minicomputer controlled by the company. This arrangement depended on individual, proprietary connections between PCs and servers. It did allow some customers and business partners to do their business with a given enterprise, and for a decade, it looked like the future. IBM's market share and reputation continued to shrink.

But at the end of the 1990s, a new opportunity opened up. The Microsoft architecture allowed mostly in-enterprise interaction and occasional one-on-one interactions between a customer and a single company. The web offered more. Its open architecture was available to any customer and any company, promising integration among everyone seamlessly across the world. Websites put together in a simple computer language that almost anyone could learn began popping up everywhere. Customers found it easy and exciting to use the new universal browsers to visit those websites and, before long, to do business on them. Microsoft's approach suddenly looked obsolete. IBM's software business was in bad shape by then, but this new disruption offered a chance to leapfrog the competition. If only IBM could figure out how to seize the opportunity.

The large businesses and governments that were still IBM's core clients now needed to respond to their own customers, who were demanding self-service marketplaces. IBM's customers' customers wanted to manage their bank accounts and buy consumer goods, airline tickets, insurance, and so on, without having to walk into a store and talk to an employee sitting at a terminal. They wanted the freedom to do their business at their own convenience, day or night.

As consumers became accustomed to using browsers to conduct transactions, IBM's enterprise customers had no choice but to create web-based solutions and to offer their customers the tools they needed to build web-based functionality. They could see the future well enough to know that without these functions they'd be shunted into the slow lane.

Although IBM had the world's experts in mainframe tools dealing with high-volume transactions and databases, it did not have, or even have the ability to create, products that customers needed to grab onto the web. In terms of competition, the only good news was that the leaders in pre-web, client–server technology didn't either.

Inside IBM, many people naturally looked at this problem incrementally (informatively). They believed they could adopt necessary technology and skills (principally a new computer language called Java from Sun Microsystems) and develop extensions to the mainframe tools they were already selling. They found allies in their customers' own development shops—people IBM had worked with for years who were comfortable with IBM tools. In the IBMers' minds there was clear, compelling evidence for this incremental approach based on surveys and direct interaction with counterparts at client companies. Just like Humminbird's market researchers prior to the arrival of Sue Symons, they were asking the wrong people the wrong questions, and only seeing what they were already expecting to see.

Danny knew that this was the wrong approach, but without a common language of not nots and authentic demand, the reasons were tough to get across. So instead, he and his colleagues struggled and fought internal battles, like the one in that auditorium in North Carolina. They were lucky that the core authentic demand was clearly in view. Another thing in their favor was that the structure of the business wasn't changing. Internet or not, IBM was still selling to large enterprises and governments with many customers. These organizations still needed tools and solutions for managing data; the same people in the same roles were still their customers.

Danny was one of the most traveled people at IBM. He made a habit of going out talking to customers. Of course the salespeople did that too, but sales conversations usually stuck to well-worn paths and didn't deviate. Danny tried to hold conversations that let new things come up. In this case he had noticed something weird. Of course his customers—software development departments and large companies—talked about software and about their technical requirements. But they added something that didn't fit the usual discussion. They were telling Danny, consistently, that they weren't able to hire Java programmers. Java was cool. A new generation of programmers wanted to work with it. They weren't interested in learning about and working with IBM's old COBOL-based tools.

The three key members of the executive team, Danny, John Swainson, and Steve Mills, intuitively realized that the approach of simply extending old-line mainframe tools to incorporate Java wouldn't work. There was an emerging value chain, stretching from consumers, to companies that sold to them, to web-centric developers (in-house and third party), to the tools those developers needed to build their systems, and finally to IBM. The shift to the internet, and recognition of what could be done on the web, were taking place at every level of that value chain. They represented comprehensive changes that couldn't be addressed incrementally. But at the same time, they had to be addressed realistically, in ways that took into account the not nots of every significant stakeholder.

The WebSphere team dealt with this tangle of issues piece by piece over a period of at least four years. In retrospect, a not not approach would have clarified the situation into a chain of not nots (as illustrated in figure 5.1), similar to the parable of how for the want of a nail a kingdom was lost.

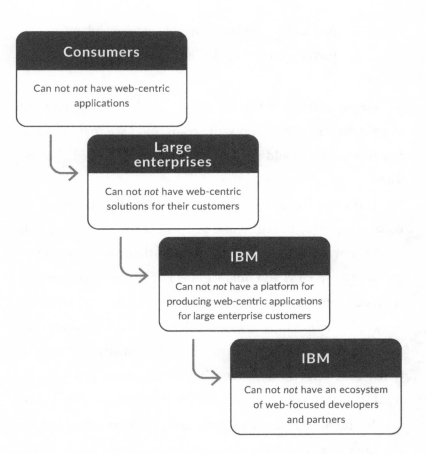

Figure 5.1. Not *not* waterfall

1. Not having consumers use your web solutions was not OK.

2. Not having web-centric solutions to attract those consumers was not OK.

3. Not having a platform for developers to generate those solutions was not OK.

4. Not having an ecosystem of developers and
partners using that platform wasn't OK either.

Danny didn't have this vocabulary, but by parsing out what were effectively the not nots, the team could see that informative innovation would not get them where they needed to go. They needed a transformation.

This chain links (1) the authentic demand of the ultimate consumers to (2) the authentic demand of the enterprises that serve them to (3) the authentic demand that those enterprises required from IBM and finally to (4) IBM's authentic demand from developers and partners. You can see each of the four tiers as people maintaining a grip on their habitual situations. In a web-enabled world, a consumer will normally buy a plane ticket, rent a hotel room, deposit a check, stream a movie, and do dozens of other things through the web. It's simply not OK for them to rush off at lunch hour to the travel agency or the bank, not OK for them to check a newspaper to see what's playing at a local movie theater, find a map to figure out how to drive to that theater, and so on. The world has changed, and it would be strange for most people most of the time to behave in the old way. So, accordingly, the large enterprises that provide seats on airplanes, rooms in hotels, banking, entertainment, and navigation can't maintain a grip on doing what they do without providing web apps to their customers. So, in turn, IBM can't maintain a grip on selling to those customers unless they offer a platform for building web applications for doing these things.

Back in the conference room with the lab director yelling that he'd do it his way, Danny saw this chain of not nots clearly enough to know that the guy's plan wouldn't work. IBM's success depended on leveraging—joining, really—an ecosystem of young Java programmers and open-source server gurus to achieve the second, *transformative* type of innovation. There was plenty of programming talent at IBM, but the incremental, informational innovation they were capable of wasn't right for the job. That's why Danny cut the budget for that approach.

To effect this transformation and create a web business, Danny and his colleagues assessed the strengths, needs, and focus of the emerging ecosystem. There was IBM, with its legacy systems built around mainframes, still prevalent in large-enterprise solutions. There were Microsoft's developer tools, which were preeminent in client–server solutions, tools the web was quickly making obsolete. There was Sun Microsystem's Java, which had traction among developers as the cool, easy way to build web apps. There was also the emergence of open-source tools, such as the Apache web server, which were rapidly proliferating in those cool developer circles but were loosely managed and not acceptable to large enterprises.

What the WebSphere team did, in effect, was to look at these loosely coupled situations in terms of the not nots that were hemming in each institution. For each one of them, those not nots added up to a predicament, an unacceptable situation in which the participants were stuck. The job, for IBM and its key partners, was to engineer ways for each party to escape from those predicaments. The WebSphere team implemented an approach to connect the dots and position IBM for the web-based future.

The reality was that there was no master plan and no explicit not not reasoning, but in hindsight the disparate pieces all fit together:

- Sun had what IBM didn't: a growing ecosystem of eager developers who went to Java parties and wore Java T-shirts and eagerly programmed Java apps. IBM didn't have and couldn't generate that kind of cool. However, Sun's leaders knew that the real money was in the large-enterprise systems—IBM's stock and trade— and they couldn't sell in that world without IBM. The answer here was partnership.

- Apache was the premier web server architecture on the market, and it was free. Large enterprises couldn't use it; it didn't offer the kind of licensing or support that they required. IBM knew how to fix that. IBM funded the Apache nonprofit organization, helped it create the kind of licenses that enterprise customers needed, and made it all available, still free. IBM wasn't accustomed to giving stuff away for free, but the WebSphere team became convinced that as Apache turned into a standard among its customers, there would be plenty to sell. This decision was particularly noteworthy because there was an IBM team working hard to build a proprietary web server to compete with Apache. After a tough internal battle, IBM abandoned the in-house effort and went with the emerging free standard.

- Programmers needed development platforms like Microsoft's award-winning and popular tool, Visual Studio (VS). But for IBM, VS had two strikes against it: it belonged to a competitor, and it was oriented toward older pre-web architectures. That gave IBM an opening, and it created Eclipse as an open-source competitor, a developer alternative. Eclipse wasn't initially as good as VS, but with the connection to cool technology like Apache and Java, it was the equipment that served the authentic demand. The developer community around the open-source project flourished and continuously made it better. Given Java's cool factor and the availability of free open-source tools (Apache and Eclipse), students in universities quickly flocked to them, graduating as a new crop of young programmers who were already familiar with them and dealing a solid blow to the competition for web solutions and tools.

In aggregate, IBM's entry into the web space required the company to transform its culture. It had to collaborate instead of acting like the biggest kid on the block, selling everything it made (not giving it away) and making everything it sold. This was the first time in the company's then eighty-plus-year history that IBM leveraged open-source offerings and recognized their potential relevance to the enterprise market. It was the first time that IBM devised relationships like the ones with Sun and the Apache organization. Steve Mills provided executive leadership and corporate cover. John and Danny used their business and technical teams to drive the evolution of WebSphere and the core of Eclipse into the market. All in all, it was a successful, multifaceted innovation, responding to an interconnected web of not nots and providing IBM and its partners access to new opportunities.

The transformation was a success. As we noted earlier, over ten years the WebSphere brand grew to $8 billion in annual revenue, with IBM leading the segment in profitability.

In contrast to the GMR situation, the story of WebSphere is one of an opportunity (and risk) that IBM saw and capitalized on, because the people in charge correctly saw transformation as the right path. However, without the language and tools of not nots and authentic demand, the transformation led to more conflict, wasted money, and wasted time. Fights broke out because people saw things from their own perspective and lacked a common framework for thinking through the issues together. Danny made a judgment call based on instinct. Luckily for IBM, two things went right: his judgment happened to be the right one, and he and his partners were able to win the internal battles to implement it.

A common framework involves more than a common language; it's a common way to notice and investigate the phenomena at hand and to use the results of that investigation to decide on and go ahead with a particular kind of innovation.

Challenges to Transformative Innovation

Transformative change requires dealing with a very particular set of challenges centered around the problem of people's psychological immunity to change. Because transformations are changes that can ripple across whole systems, management-level people are usually the ones who have the opportunity to see systems as a whole and attempt to change them in transformative ways. But when transformations require people to do their jobs differently, or even think of their jobs differently, they often respond with a kind of immune response, fighting off the change in subtle and hidden ways so that the transformation never takes root. Some of the best managers for informative innovation don't have the right orientation or set of skills to lead effectively in a transformative context.

At IBM it was commonplace for people to worry that any time there was a new idea, the "IBM antibodies" would rush out to kill it. Resistance to transformative change can be explicit, or it can go on behind the backs of management. It can be noticeable as a sort of anxiety, or it can be unconscious and barely noticeable even to the people doing the resisting. As William Ouchi recognized with his Theory Z, conscious and unconscious fears about losing one's job can generate that sort of antibody.[1] But explicit fear about losing a job is just the tip of the iceberg.

Take the example we mentioned earlier of a railroad transforming into a transportation company. From the boardroom it might look like a great idea. By reimagining their railroad company as a transportation company, the board members and senior leadership can imagine leveraging in-house expertise in logistics and customer relationships to address opportunities in shipping and air freight. In other words, they see that the company has assets and expertise that give the company a "right of way" into a bigger market. And a bigger market means more money and success, potentially for all stakeholders in the company. By contrast, Sharon, the executive who owns the profit-and-loss business of shipping fruit by rail, may cheer the idea at all-hands meetings, but in conversations with her team may express private doubts about the company's ability to execute the vision. Sharon's immune response has been triggered, and (maybe even unconsciously) she slow-walks the changes required in her division. Multiply this modest bit of sand in the gears by the number of people like Sharon and you can see the magnitude of the problem of getting from the vision to the realization.

The result can be gridlock, a thousand little instances of "I can't do X because of Y." Clearing the gridlock is doable; Danny's success with WebSphere is an example of successful transformation, but the number of conflicts that arise and the extra time and effort needed to resolve them are almost always underestimated.

Immunities are triggered when people react to an imposed change by experiencing it as a threat to some commitment they have. If they were to behave in the way the transformation calls for, they wouldn't be true to themselves in some sense. Tracking down what that sense is, in each case, is no easy task. People might be committed to keeping their job—the point Ouchi made in *Theory Z*. Or they might be committed to seeing themselves as competent. Maybe Sharon is committed to being true to her word; she can make a promise to her rail customers about getting their fruit to them on time, but isn't sure she can make the same promise to air freight customers and keep it. Or perhaps Sharon is committed to staying within her insurance budget, and she doesn't have enough experience with the air freight insurance market to feel confident on that score. People's commitments are idiosyncratic and individual. And they can be hidden just as the ways they resist violating those commitments can be hidden.

It is almost always easier and cheaper to figure out how to avoid triggering immunities than to power through, attempting to force people into new behaviors and roles. But the kind of work required to figure out how to avoid triggering immunities is not well recognized or trained for, nor is the ability to do this work a common skill set in the management of these kinds of innovative changes.

Because immunity to change is such a central challenge for transformative innovation, the kind of leadership it requires differs from management of more conventional situations. Normal managers essentially manage toward situational stability in the face of change. They adapt to external threats in order to maintain or enhance their or their company's position in that stable market. The leadership skills needed for transformative change aren't about keeping things stable but about keeping people on track when the innovation goal is to destabilize the situation. Even great managers can be bad at this. Transformative leaders pay attention to the psychological challenges of transformation. They help people avoid triggers or deal with them, in order to overcome implicit or explicit resistance to the changes the company plans to effect.

CHAPTER 6
Formative Innovation: SoulCycle and a Strip Mall

Informative innovation *fills up* a company's existing culture and form with new products, methods, and assets. Think railroads that innovate by adding refrigerators cars (or think GMR at IBM). Transformative innovation *changes* the culture or form, to tackle threats and opportunities that are outside the scope of the original form. Think railroads that transform into transportation companies (or think WebSphere). Formative innovation takes place when you don't have a form to begin with and need to create it from scratch. Formative innovation is usually associated with disruptive startups, but established companies can also create new formative businesses, as some of today's large businesses are attempting with block-chain and large-language-model technologies.

But where to start? Startups usually begin with an idea. Some entrepreneurially minded person notices something that looks like a problem and has an inspiration about a solution. Or a technically minded person sees a new technology and has an inspiration about how it can be used. As described earlier, these inspirations almost never result in successful companies. It's telling that even in the very select group of startups that do succeed, nearly all of them succeed on the basis of a product that was not their first idea. Inspiration can shock people into action—into quitting their job and starting a business, for example. But the evidence is that inspiration is not reliable as the founding idea of a company.

The two most popular alternatives to the pure-inspiration approach both have roots in Silicon Valley. Human-centered design got started at Stanford in the 1950s and caught fire as "design thinking" with Tom Kelly, Stanford's D School, and Ideo about a decade ago. Lean startup began with Steve Blank's *Four Steps to the Epiphany*[1] in the early 2000s and was further developed and popularized by Eric Reis.

Design thinking and lean startup are each based on sound principles. Design thinking emphasizes solving problems by focusing on the psychologies, emotions, and physical constraints of the users. Lean startup emphasizes talking with customers and rapidly iterating on products until there's evidence of demand, as a prelude to building actual products. Both are now rich systems with lots of extensions and elaborations. There are reams of books and online materials, templates, classes, experts, and practitioners involved with each. But neither approach offers a coherent view of authentic demand. Design thinking starts with a prompt—an assumption that there will be demand for an appropriate solution to a predefined problem. Lean startup systems seek evidence of demand without defining what it is.

Formative innovation—creating new forms—works by reorganizing how a situation is perceived and by inserting something (often a product) into the situation that exposes customers' unmet authentic demands and frees people to meet them. Formative innovations frequently leverage rights of way. An established company may have rights of way in the form of technology, know-how, patents, distribution channels, brand value, or other assets it can leverage for a formative innovation.

In the Humminbird Fish Finder example, the reorganization entailed a conceptual shift in understanding the customer from "recreational *fisherman*" to "*recreational* fisherman." The product was a fish-finding device built to meet the recreational needs of people on a fishing excursion. The rights of way were the company's brand value and all of its assets, which gave Humminbird a claim to selling things for fishing boats.

Another example of right of way involved Matt's father and his strip mall outside Philadelphia. Over a period of years, he did everything he could think of to improve the business. He improved the buildings, added parking spots, made special deals with anchor tenants that he thought would attract more business, and put up holiday decorations and improved the signage. All these things were along the lines of informative innovation.

Then one day a representative from a cell phone carrier came knocking. It turned out that the mall happened to be located on a hill in a good location. The carrier wanted rights to place a cell phone tower on the roof. Matt's father recognized that there was a whole new form available for his business. Before long there were cell towers for all the carriers on that roof, and also satellite dishes. It was a whole new business built on the roof of the existing one.

Formative innovations involve new, creative ways to look at the assets of a business and use them to create new businesses or business lines. Something like this actually happened with the railroad business in the late nineteenth century. Rapidly growing telegraph and (later) telephone companies needed to string wires along the routes between urban centers. They contracted with railroads to use their literal rights of way in land ownership for the purpose. In the case of the strip mall, the roof space and location were a metaphorical right of way for building a new business, but one that had never occurred to Matt's father.

Formative innovation usually starts small, but it isn't incremental like the informative variety. It's the core innovation for disruptive startups. It can evade the common problem of growth or returns slowing down when technologies or companies become more mature (the so-called S-curve). Formative innovations can also evade the immunities to change that kick in whenever businesses attempt transformative innovation. A formative business can be so new and different that it doesn't trigger resistance; it's usually driven by a new or nonthreatening part of an organization.

Formative innovations are Plan A for most disruptive startups, but rarer events for mature companies. Brand-new startups, though, don't have railroad rights of way across the country, or even strip mall roofs. What they have is the time, attention, creativity, skills, networks, and efforts of their founders; these have to serve as rights of way.

SoulCycle:
Building a New Company on a New Form

In the early 2000s, the fitness industry was at a turning point. It had taken off decades earlier, with weightlifting and Arnold Schwarzenegger and Gold's Gym holding up one wing while Jane Fonda, Richard Simmons, and the aerobics craze supporting the other. The business model for these centers was essentially to sell annual memberships and then minimize costs. Where memberships were all-inclusive, group fitness classes were cost centers. At best, group fitness was a separate P&L with a manager very focused on costs. As a result, the classes tended to be mediocre or worse. The instructors were poorly paid and had to stitch together careers running from center to center.

By 2005, the big franchise fitness center trend was waning. Julie Rice and Elizabeth Cutler had met in a spin class in New York, and together with their spin instructor decided to try something different. They started their own boutique, which they called SoulCycle.[2]

Spinning was getting popular, and that helped. But Julie and Elizabeth didn't believe that the particular fitness activity was the key issue. Working out was an experience. But most people saw exercise, particularly aerobic exercise, as a bad experience. It was something you had to endure in order to reach health or attractiveness goals. That's what made health club memberships a seasonal business, with most sales made in January, following New Year's resolutions.

While others in the industry assumed they understood the demand, Julie and Elizabeth saw through that. In a formative move, they realized that they could create a new kind of business by making aerobic exercise into something people, and particularly women, authentically demanded, turning it from an activity customers endured to one they sought out. With Humminbird, Sue Symons—an outsider—was the one to see the demand. For GMR, the demand was belatedly uncovered via an unexpected reaction by a reporter from *Byte* magazine. Matt's dad got a knock on the door from a cell tower salesman. Elizabeth and Julie noticed an authentic demand on their own, most likely because it was their own demand.

As it was for Humminbird, seeing the authentic demand can be like discovering a compass. For SoulCycle, the first step was to change the business model. Julie and Elizabeth saw that the common franchise fitness center business model undermined the product by casting it as a cost center. By eliminating annual membership fees in favor of pay-per-class, they shifted from a business that only paid lip service to filling up classes to one that depended on it.

Next, to meet the authentic demand they recognized, Julie and Elizabeth needed employees who wanted to be there and who were interested in helping their customers want to be there. That cost money. They decided to pay their instructors well, to offer them health care and days off and other perks. In turn, the instructors had to take ownership of the classes. They put together their own music playlists, practiced their patter, got to know their clients, and shaped the spinning sequences to fit their regulars. They showed up with fresh energy to each class. Julie and Elizabeth decided not to instruct classes themselves, partly to focus on the business and partly to discourage competition among instructors. They doubled down on avoiding competition, letting instructors know the job was not only to fill up their own classes but to fill up the classes before and after theirs too.

Next, they focused on the experience itself. The front lobbies at most gyms were imposing desks where people stood in line to have their membership credentials checked. SoulCycle turned theirs into welcoming, brightly lit hospitality centers. But the heart of the experience was on the bikes.

SoulCycle clients passed through the hospitality center entrance into a darkened studio, as though they were going into a theater. The temperature, the music, the dim lights, the fact that the leader was also riding, how close the bikes were set up next to each other—all those features were meant to do everything possible for the cyclists to have a profound experience.

On a bumpy bus ride in Nairobi, of all places, Matt asked Elizabeth about her secret: What made SoulCycle such a breakout success? Her answer was that people need to get out of themselves; they need a time, even just for five minutes, when their everyday lives fall away and they can live in the moment. When they experience that, and know it's available to them, they'll keep coming back.

SoulCycle is a model of formative innovation. Why do people exercise? The illusion rampant in the fitness marketplace was that people exercised to keep fit or look better. That answer made so much sense that it rarely occurred to anyone to ask the question again. The sense that it made was further confirmed by the evidence people noticed, such as the seasonality in sales of gym memberships.

But by seeing through the illusions and re-asking the question, Julie and Elizabeth were able to reorganize the situation. They noticed the pesky, mostly ignored fact that people sometimes enjoyed exercising; they sometimes got something out of the experience itself. By taking that peripheral, ignored fact and making it central to the business, they reorganized the situation and drew a new conceptual outline around what a fitness boutique could be. Similar to how Jim Balkcom reorganized his thinking around fish finders and reformed Humminbird's business, Julie and Elizabeth formed a brand-new business by reorganizing the market in their heads. Before SoulCycle, Julie Rice was a talent agent and Elizabeth Cutler was a real estate broker. Their only rights of way into the fitness business were their time, attention, creativity, skills, networks, and efforts.

When SoulCycle launched, there were only a few small fitness boutiques, mostly yoga studios or private gyms built around a popular instructor. SoulCycle broke open the boutique fitness business, taking it to sixty studios in fourteen cities before selling the company to Equinox.

Now Julie and Elizabeth are on to new adventures.

Challenges to Formative Innovation

Remember Patrick Swayze in the movie *Ghost*? The poor guy has been murdered and his wife's in danger, but he can't do anything about it because he's a ghost. He's desperate to make himself heard, to make a difference, to right a terrible wrong, to save his wife from a terrible danger. But no one can see him or hear him. That's what it can feel like to be a formative innovator. Not at first, of course. At first, it feels as though the world is your oyster. But as you try to accomplish things that actually require other people—investors, customers—that positive feeling fades away.

The biggest problem when creating a new form is being stuck in the world of ghosts. You and your innovation are not being drawn into the world. As smart, energetic, and diligent as you may be, the hard truth is that it's not up to you to be welcomed; other people have to do it. You have to be let in. You start with a fantasy that people will flock to what you're doing; it'll be either love at first sight or at worst a process of educating customers about how your innovation will improve their lives. Like Joe Reger at Springbot (whom we met in chapter 1), we have a hefty to-do list—logos to create, important people to meet, software to debug, pro forma financials to calculate. But then the ghostly reality sets in. People are already coping with their lives: customers are already buying something else, collaborators are collaborating, and investors are investing elsewhere. Your innovation is met with overwhelming indifference. It's common to swing from one extreme to another, from seeing demand everywhere to seeing it nowhere. That's a tough swing, psychologically. Plenty of innovators never go even that far; they just keep adding to the to-do list until they run out of time or money or energy, at which point they abandon the innovation and come up with an excuse (usually something about market timing).

Having made that swing is progress, but it doesn't feel like progress; it just means being face-to-face with your own Patrick Swayzeness. Take heart, though. There's certainly nonindifference out there in the marketplace; it's just hidden. The thing about formative innovation that makes it different from either trans-formative or informative is that at bottom it targets a nonindif-ference that was always present in the situation, but so far had not been noticed. Or if it had been noticed, it had been dismissed because no path to meeting it seemed possible.

The result of that not-noticing or that dismissing is that people seem not to care. And that's how nonindifference hides—camouflaged as indifference. Put it all together, and the goal of formative innovation is to find a market of people in situations where they are nonindifferent to something changing, but what that is, is usually hidden; it's not a problem they're working on. So the challenge is to distinguish the actual indifferences from the nonindifferences camouflaged as indifferences. To do that, we need to figure out where nonindifferences come from, and how they hide.

PART TWO
DELIBERATE
INNOVATION

In the situations we've looked at so far, what led to success was tracing out the implications of the not nots. The recreational fishermen who were Humminbird's customers could not *not* cope with threats to their recreation, and tracing out the implications of that not not led to new product design, distribution channels, and company culture. Buyers of hard drives could not *not* cope with threats to reliable storage and access to their data. The implications were apparent to IBM's rival, but not to IBM, which was hampered by a focus on incremental, informative innovation. The value chain around IBM's WebSphere included different constituencies that each had their not nots. Aligning them led to company success, which involved a tough struggle with other internal players who had good reasons to fight for incremental change. Soul-Cycle's customers had a not not with respect to a particular experience that's difficult to label, but nevertheless was clear enough to Elizabeth and Julie to serve as a compass for their decision-making.

Two of the most striking aspects of all those situations were (1) the not nots were hidden, and (2) figuring them out was more or less an accident. Recreational fishermen weren't busting down doors to get to entertainment devices. If they were suffering, they were suffering in silence. Hard drive buyers weren't demanding greater reliability; IBM's WebSphere customers didn't ask for open-source servers. Any complaints gym-goers had about the low quality of their spin classes were going unheard.

Sometimes customers or outsiders can see the not not that experts can't. But seeking outsider perspectives isn't a reliable approach, because much more often outsiders simply don't understand the business well enough and their ideas won't work. Even when they do have a good idea, it's rare that a business leader can hear it and get on board. Sometimes business leaders like Danny can figure out the not nots themselves through trial and error. But in either case, the leader has to have the position and character to carry through an innovation even while others in the company don't appreciate the opportunity and revert to their own agendas.

If something is (1) necessary and (2) invisible and also (3) requires a series of accidents to happen, then it won't happen very often. That itself plays a major role in innovation's enormous failure rate. Merrick and Matt's quest to change that equation and make innovation more deliberate started when they founded a company called Damballa.

CHAPTER 7
Beginning to Innovate Deliberately: The Mystery of Damballa

When Matt and Merrick started their first business together, an internet security company called Damballa, they ran into a roadblock they didn't expect. Learning to understand what happened, and listening to people persist in misunderstanding, set them on the path toward Deliberate Innovation.

Merrick was a mathematician and computer scientist before getting interested in startups. He'd been dean of the graduate program in computer science at Carnegie Mellon, and then headed up the International Computer Science Institute at UC Berkeley, before moving to Georgia Tech as undergraduate dean of the College of Computing. In between academic stints, he'd founded several companies, notably Essential Surfing Gear, the first company to provide apps for web browsing.

Merrick met Howard Schmidt when Howard came to Georgia Tech for a board meeting. Howard was the chief information security officer (CISO) at eBay. He was a motorcycle-riding grandpa who'd worked in the White House as the cybersecurity coordinator in the Executive Office of the President, where he was known as one of the foremost experts in cybersecurity, maybe before that word was even invented. After stints in government and at several large companies, he'd moved to eBay, a Silicon Valley startup that was growing spectacularly in 2005.

Merrick was excited to tell Howard about a new technology some colleagues were working on at Georgia Tech to counter what they saw as the most significant looming threat to anyone doing business on the internet. The threat didn't have a name yet either. The group at Georgia Tech was calling the threat "bot armies." The name that stuck was "botnet." The Georgia Tech team was prescient: botnets ultimately became the root cause of an enormous amount of internet fraud and online damage perpetrated by criminal enterprises and state actors.

Up until that point, computer viruses were mostly viewed as annoyances. They slowed down performance, popped up obscene messages, crashed systems. They weren't yet viewed as professionalized threats; they were irritations created by "script kiddies" who spread them mostly as malicious mischief. By contrast, botnets were composed of malware—pieces of malicious code that were designed to spread to as many computers as possible and to be as stealthy and as invisible as possible. Botnets were taking control of vast numbers of computers without their owners' knowledge. And the malware that these bots were running was becoming increasingly capable of causing their host machines to do more and more problematic things at the bidding of distant, criminal, and state-actor "botmasters." It wasn't just script kiddies anymore, but financially or politically motivated professional gangs.

Howard, of course, understood the threat early. There was a particular way that he thought the solutions that Merrick's technical partners were working on could be applied in service of the commercial interests of eBay, and he asked Merrick out to San Jose to present.

The meeting seemed like a spectacular success. Howard and his team already knew that botnets were busy ripping off eBay and its customers. Computers around the world were already impersonating humans and, for example, setting up fraudulent sellers and posting fake reviews so that buyers would trust them. Howard described this as "trust fraud." They were also subverting the advertising revenue model with fake clicks. At least as worrying as all that, bots were appearing on internal eBay computers and doing who-knew-what.

And they were ubiquitous, estimated at the time to be lodged on 17 percent of all computers worldwide. The Georgia Tech team's technology, like the GMR breakthrough and like many technologies before it, appeared to be a revolutionary solution for a huge and promising market.

Howard and his fraud team did some calculations right in front of Merrick and said, "If you can stop this kind of trust fraud, it can save eBay $40 million per year. How much will you sell it for?" Merrick, who didn't have an actual product yet, let alone a pricing plan, did what experienced entrepreneurs do—he made up a plausible number and said, "$150,000 per year or so, to start." Howard jumped on it. His next question was "How soon can you deliver?"

To the Georgia Tech team's ears and to investors' ears, when Howard said that the technology could save eBay $40 million a year in fraud, and when he asked how soon he could have it, that sure sounded like demand—it sounded to the team as though eBay was going to be a customer that thought help was finally at hand.

Howard wasn't the only potential customer who had this sort of excited reaction to the promise of the technology. The Georgia Tech team heard similar things from dozens of other prospective companies. Right out of the gate, it was selling a rudimentary data feed to a large security company for $100k per year.

With eBay's apparent interest in becoming the first big customer, and other potential customers signing contracts and otherwise signaling interest, it never occurred to us (Merrick and Matt) that we were stuck. We were clearly off to a good start with marketing and sales, one of the four categories discussed in chapter 1. The other three we thought we needed to address were technology, team, and financing. On the technology front, we got to work securing IP rights from Georgia Tech and turning the work that had been done into a functional product. On the team front, Merrick decided to act as our initial CEO, and we started looking for others to carry the company forward. We put together a slide deck and started talking to investors, quickly raising $2.5 million on a $5 million valuation (considered remarkable at the time). The two VC funds that participated also helped us with building the team.

Six months later, Damballa was ready with a product for eBay. We showed up more or less asking, "Who should we talk to next, and where does everyone sign?" The team had done what it thought was its part and was ready for eBay to follow through. But very strangely, there did not seem to be a lot of interest in actually having anything happen. Howard delegated the project. There were polite conversations that never led anywhere. Damballa survived, but never sold a trust fraud or click fraud solution to eBay, or to anyone else, for that matter.

Our model of how the world worked didn't include serious corporate CISOs just sneezing at solutions that could save $40 million (and growing) lost to fraud. Our view was that companies are in the business of making a profit by increasing their top lines and reducing their costs. Here was a technology that promised to do just that, and the person in charge of buying thought it would be an important fix. We thought the same, and had other potential customers saying the same kind of thing.

Everyone at Damballa believed that all the elements that made up demand were in place. The product would save customers a large amount of money, it worked the way they needed it to, and we had a competent team and sufficient capital to operate. Most important, we all had a fixed idea in our heads that we never questioned: companies would not tolerate their machines being compromised. Bots hiding secretly on the company computers led to all sorts of risks. Click fraud, trust fraud, stealing passwords, eavesdropping on company emails, stealing proprietary data or customer information—we made up examples, and we heard examples from people like Howard. We didn't feel stuck. Even as sales lagged expectations, we always felt that we saw the problem and could move forward by fixing it. Maybe our software increased processing time. Maybe putting third-party software like ours inside customers' firewalls was too risky for them. Maybe putting it outside their firewalls made them feel vulnerable. Maybe the particular examples of bad things bots could do weren't hitting home and we had to change the marketing.

We selected a dynamic CEO and Merrick moved himself to the board. When eBay didn't buy, and over the next several years when other sales kept falling short, internal company and board conversations all revolved around those issues. The steps the company took—replacing key management, improving the product, raising more money—were all attempts to make certain that the product, the team, the marketing and sales, and the financing were right. The company kept moving on all these fronts, eventually raising and deploying $69 million in venture capital and going through a succession of CEOs and marketing executives. But despite all the activity, Damballa was stuck.

What was missing?

As management and the board worked to get the company on track, they addressed all the conventional issues. They believed in a very clear idea of why there should be demand, and worked on the basis of that belief. They thought the customers were compromised by bots and that they would buy things to fix that—that they would not *not* buy because they couldn't allow themselves to be compromised. That view stayed at the root of all the company's plans and tactics, and it didn't budge. Internally, there were variations on that basic belief. Some people thought that money was the issue: customers would buy because being compromised cost them money. Others thought our customers would be afraid that their customers would be scared away or displaced by bots. Still others thought risk was the issue: customers would buy because they were otherwise vulnerable to fraud allegations.

With hindsight we can see that these just aren't effective ways to understand customer demand. The right question ought to have been, "What ever gave us the impression that eBay would be a customer?" On what basis did we believe that our preferred value proposition would actually drive sales?

We assumed that saving money is a reliable authentic demand; who doesn't want to save money? If our confidence in that axiom ever wavered, we could confirm it by reminding ourselves of things corporations do to save money, without recognizing that we were simply confirming a bias. In fact, if you ask nearly anyone, in any business role, what they could do to save money, there's an excellent chance they'll provide you with a list of all the things they could be doing to save money, but aren't in fact doing. The same holds for almost all the ways people usually think of what are typically called value propositions. It was starting to dawn on Merrick that some other view of what makes a customer a customer was necessary.

Through dint of hard work and tons of effort, Damballa eventually grew to $12 million in annual sales. In hindsight, it's arguable that Damballa did uncover an authentic demand, but because we never figured out its precise nature, we never understood the situations where it occurred or their frequency, so we were overoptimistic about the addressable market size. That led to financing the company unsustainably. When the company was eventually sold, all but the last round of investors lost money.

Damballa was a milestone for us. As we tried to make sense of the experience, the question of demand—how we should think about it, how we could go about discovering it—started to come into view. We didn't begin to get our arms around that question, though, until we began to notice that people we talked to about it had a very hard time even discerning the question.

CHAPTER 8
Contending with the Waking Dream

We were surprised by Howard's lack of interest in buying from Damballa. We were baffled by the continuing lack of sales as we did what we thought was solving one customer problem after another—even when the customers had clearly stated a problem and we objectively solved it. Even after Damballa was sold at a loss, the mystery of it stayed with us. As we continued our lives, Merrick grappled with trying to explain value propositions to the students in his entrepreneurship classes. After all, Damballa's value proposition had seemed airtight—compelling to eBay, to ourselves, to investors, to other potential customers. Both Merrick and Matt were constantly talking with fellow investors, startup founders, and people with various business ideas. It was like déjà vu—all of their value propositions seemed just as airtight and obvious to them. Everyone seemed eager to either convince us or seek assurance that they were right about their value proposition. We started to feel as though we were living in a waking dream. Everyone was talking about an important thing as though they knew what they were talking about, and they were all agreeing with one another. Even when they disagreed, they held to the same way of thinking and set of assumptions. One person would say, "They'll buy this product because it will save them money," and a critic would argue that it would break too easily or wasn't attractive enough or was too heavy, and customers wouldn't buy it for that reason. They were talking in circles.

None of that seemed connected to the reality we'd experienced with Damballa, or the reality we started to notice all around us, of startups with seemingly compelling value propositions that turned out to be mirages, ultimately yielding nothing but indifference from customers. There were a million arguments and beliefs about what would sell or about market size that rarely correlated with what actually sold or in what volume.

Merrick's breakthrough on this (Matt was convinced) came not so much from his experience with startups but from his experience as a mathematician. Merrick started to see all sorts of value propositions as essentially the same—members of a single type. What value propositions all had in common was a positive structure; they all made assertions about what some group of people would do because of some property of a product or service connected to some property the people possessed. That value proposition structure didn't seem to connect with the real world. In the real world, people are actors; they're not bundles of properties. And the things (including products and services) that they interact with only have meaning with respect to how people are going about being who they are. Consequently, you simply could not depend on customers or clients to buy things because those things had a property, such as "pretty cheap," that connected to a property of the customer, such as "penny pincher." That sort of logic just didn't work, at least not consistently.

Once Merrick noticed that, it was just a short step to turning value propositions upside down. If you couldn't connect to how customers and clients actually behaved by using positive arguments, could you use negative ones? If you couldn't predict what people would do, could you predict what they would not *not* do?

Before Merrick was an entrepreneur or a computer scientist or a mathematician, he was a magician. In high school he'd earned pin money doing magic shows at kids' birthday parties. So he thought of a card trick.

Imagine a magician on a stage. They pick out someone in the audience, look them in the eye, and say, "You sir, what's your name?" The man says, "Jim." The magician says, "Jim, thanks for coming tonight. Will you please stand up?" Jim stands up. The magician says, "Everyone, give Jim a round of applause!" then after the applause, "Jim, can you come up here on stage and pick a card for me?" The magician fans out a deck of cards, and Jim dutifully trots up to the stage and picks one.

This scenario might not look like much, but for a professional magician it's practically life or death. If they can't consistently, night after night, get absolute strangers—people who may hate being the center of attention—to stand up in front of an audience and pick a card, then the magician's out of a job. They don't do it by offering any value to Jim; there's no value proposition here. Instead, they have figured out a particular sequence of steps where each one throws an individual and the whole audience into a new situation. For Jim, it may feel something like this: "The magician looked me in the eye and asked my name, so I said it. Then they asked me to stand up and everyone was looking at me, so I stood up. Then they said, 'It'll be easy, just come on stage and pick a card,' so I went and picked one."

Jim doesn't articulate these things to himself; he just copes with each new situation in the way that people do. But night after night the show depends on it, and someone always comes up on stage to pick a card. An established professional magician is, in that way, like an established company that can depend on customers buying. To get there they had to notice the anatomy of each situation. Maybe if they didn't get Jim's name first, he wouldn't stand up, or maybe the name step isn't necessary at all. Perhaps if Jim weren't standing up, he might balk at coming down to the stage. Perhaps the applause matters, or maybe it doesn't. Each situation had to be noticed and sussed out with respect to the things that people like Jim could do, and then it has to be shaped *to eliminate the things he might do that do not lead to his picking a card.*

Figuring this out with respect to an innovation is very different from devising a value proposition like "I'll get someone down to the stage to pick a card by . . . [for example, telling them they'll enjoy it or offering a prize]." There's a logic to the sequence that we could describe positively after the fact. But before the fact, there's no road map to constructing the sequence, nothing to distinguish between a sequence that works and one that doesn't.

The insight that value propositions don't work for innovation and that something else might seemed very important to Merrick and Matt. But people listened to them talk about this insight, nodded, and kept making up stories. At that point Merrick was on the board at Damballa, when the company was stumbling and everyone was making up stories about how to set things right. He kept telling them to stop, but it was like one of those dreams where you can't make yourself heard. The positive value proposition model—"Customers will do X because of Y," or its corollary "They're not doing X [buying] because we didn't do Y"—seemed to have enchanted everyone. They were satisfied with this way of thinking, and Merrick's questions and protests just did not compute. It was during that time, as we (Merrick and Matt) tried to make sense of what was going wrong with Damballa and other companies we'd experienced, that we started asking ourselves: What are these stories? What is this waking dream?

That line of questioning led to research and conversations and then collaborations with behavioral economists and decision theorists who'd been working on exactly these sorts of issues. Ironically, some of the pioneers in decision theory had been at Carnegie Mellon, doing their early experiments just one building away from where Merrick had been a young professor. He'd paid no attention to them then. But now, thanks to a mathematician's insight, he came to see the value of their approach.

Over years of working with subsequent cohorts at Flashpoint, we learned to be wary of a whole set of cognitive illusions and biases, which we came to think of as the waking dream. They're not individual faults and weaknesses; they're integral parts of the human psyche. They're our umwelt.

The Umwelt

In 1909, a zoologist named Jakob Johann von Uexküll took the German word for environment, *umwelt*, and gave it a particular meaning. In biology umwelt now means not just an animal's surroundings or environment but the part of the surroundings that the animal can sense and experience. You can't smell many of the odors your dog smells, so they're not part of your umwelt. The dog, with his dichromatic eyes, can't see red as a separate color, so it doesn't exist in his umwelt. The odorant molecules the dog can sense, and the wavelengths that stimulated your optic nerve, in fact surround both of you. But our senses capture only a slice of what's really out there.

For people the umwelt isn't just a sensory issue; it's also a conceptual one. The things people see and notice depend not only on our physical senses but also on our social senses. We hear the sound of people speaking a foreign language, but we're deaf to what they're saying. Walk into a barbershop and the barber will notice your hair and probably be blind to your shoes; walk into a shoe store and the salesperson might not see your hair but will notice your shoes. We constantly make sense of the world around us, based on our sensory inputs but also on our culture, knowledge, and situation. We combine those things effortlessly, almost instantaneously, to understand what's going on around us. Imagine walking past a park bench and noticing a woman talking into a banana as though it were a telephone. What sense would you make of that scene? Now take a few more steps and notice a toddler next to her, also talking into a banana. Your sensemaking sense probably just turned on a dime.

When we make sense of things, we're necessarily excluding other possibilities. Human beings can't function without sensemaking, but excluding elements of our environment can also be dangerous. Those chemicals the dog might smell but you can't could be poisonous. Those cultures that treat racial inferiority as if it were a natural fact persist in the face of all contrary evidence. For each of us, our umwelt is something like a waking dream. Seeing through the biases and cognitive illusions that separate the world we imagine we live in from the world we really inhabit isn't just a healthy exercise—it's an enormous opportunity for innovation. But doing this is not easy, because we don't notice that we're not noticing things.

Until Sue Symons spoke up, the people at Humminbird never noticed that recreation was at least as important as fishing was for their customers. It was there in their description of those customers as recreational fishermen, but they saw right through it. Even in the act of asking customers what they wanted ("What features would you really like to see in a fish finder?"), they were just seeking and receiving confirmation of their biases and illusions. The same thing happened when IBM launched its GMR disks. The inventors of the new technology, and the marketing people around them, were sure customers wanted disks with greater areal density, and no doubt the customers would have said so too. The authentic demand was hidden from them both until Patterson pulled that disk out of the server and revealed the authentic demand for reliability. And even then, EMC listened, but IBM didn't. During the conflicts at IBM over WebSphere, the people opposed to Danny's plans weren't oblivious to Java. They just saw it as one more feature customers were asking for—something they could engineer. So they noticed it in a way that allowed them to not notice it.

Seeing through the limitations of our umwelts and the biases and misdirections of our psyches is an important move toward more accurately perceiving real not nots and the authentic demands they entail. You can't notice what you don't notice, but if you know something about how people generally distort things, you can take steps to watch out for the blind spots, in yourself and in others.

The next sections will focus on four of the biggest issues that get in the way for innovators:

- The curse of knowledge
- The lure of features
- Fundamental attribution bias
- Confirmation bias

The Curse of Knowledge

Our brains are practically Olympic athletes at the sport of jumping to conclusions. Give your brain the tiniest bit of information and it'll hand you back a fully formed opinion. Don't believe me? Quick, answer this question in your head:

Elizabeth is intelligent and strong. Will she be a good leader?

Did "yes" or "probably" pop into your head? Now try it again:

Elizabeth is intelligent and strong and corrupt and cruel. Will she be a good leader?

If you're like most people most of the time, you didn't pause before thinking up an answer to the first question. You didn't ask yourself, *What would I actually need to know in order to decide whether I think Elizabeth would make a good leader?* In fact, when you read the second question and realized it was a trick, you probably still came up with a conclusion—maybe "Definitely not; she'd be a tyrant" or "Still yes; good leaders don't have to be nice guys." In either case, you probably *still* didn't stop before making your decision to wonder about what information might constitute sufficient grounds for a decision about Elizabeth and her leadership prospects.

When we think quickly, we think mostly by association. We've got associations with the words *intelligent* and *strong*, and the usual procedure is to conjure up those associations and make a decision based on them. The missing information contained in *corrupt and cruel* were absent, so there was no opportunity to conjure up associations about them. As a consequence, answering an important question about leadership based on just two adjectives feels perfectly OK. What's true about Elizabeth is true in general. Our waking moments are full to the brim with opinions and orientations and views based on inadequate information that somehow felt perfectly adequate. This is called the *curse of knowledge*. We're cursed to assume that whatever knowledge we have is enough.[1]

The curse of knowledge messes with our attempting to uncover not nots mostly through our overconfidence. Innovators form opinions before they know it, and never think to question them. When they talk to customers, they're wildly overconfident that they're asking the right questions, that they're communicating to the potential customer accurately, and that they're understanding the customer's answers correctly. Jim Balkcom already knew why people bought fish finders, Elizabeth Cutler's competitors already knew why people went to the gym, and Matt's dad already knew how to rent out space in a strip mall. Formative innovations are based on new discoveries of not nots and nonindifferences, but how can you discover something new when you've already explained things to yourself, without even noticing?

The Lure of Features

In the marketing world, there are ongoing discussions of features versus benefits. Features are functionalities or attributes of a product or service. It has a handle or doesn't; they deliver to your door or they don't. Benefits are the value that the customer gets from the product or service, at least in the eyes of the marketing department. The feature is a handle; the benefit is that it's easier to hold. (The link between a feature and a benefit is often called an *affordance*. Products are said to have features that afford benefits.)

In the innovation world, what benefits a customer is a big question, but it leads to a bigger one: Is thinking in terms of benefits the best way to predict how customers will respond? (Spoiler alert: probably not.) What is clear, though, is that there's

a psychological tendency to think in terms of features and benefits, which gets in the way of identifying authentic demand. At
Flashpoint, one way we reminded ourselves to avoid this tendency
was through a meme. Our go-to term for product was *mud pie*; we
used it to invoke the following story:

Imagine a hard-working mom coming home at the end of a
long, stressful day at work. Her daughter, the cutest little girl you
ever saw, comes running out of the garden holding a mud pie in
her hands. "Look what I made for you, Mommy! I made you a
mud pie!" A smile breaks across her mother's face. "It's so beautiful, sweetie! It's perfect; I love it. It's exactly what I wanted!"

Both the little girl and her mother are being authentic. The
little girl thought hard about what her mom would like, and she
made the mud pie with love. Her mom saw that mud pie and
tears came to her eyes. But should the little girl think that other
mothers in the neighborhood want mud pies? Should she think
her mom will want one tomorrow?

Products are mud pies. The role their features play is shaped
and revealed by the situation. Thinking of features or benefits
doesn't shed light on authentic demand. A handle may in fact
make the product easier to hold, but there may be no unmet
authentic demand for "easier to hold."

The mud pie story also warns of something else. The little
girl and her mother responded to the mud pie authentically—
they really loved it. The authenticity is a warning for innovators
looking for authentic demand. The nominal goal of talking to
customers is to uncover demand, and to do that by asking people

questions and showing them products. Positive answers and positive reactions to the products are supposed to validate the innovator's thesis about what the market wants or needs. But, as the story makes obvious, responses, even compelling emotional reactions, don't reveal the object of the demand.

Fundamental Attribution Bias

Fundamental attribution bias is one of the better-studied cognitive biases. It is in play when you see someone's behavior and mistakenly attribute it to their personality. Someone cuts you off on the road and you think, "What a jerk." But if you cut someone off on the road, you might think, "Whoops, I didn't see him" or "Sorry, but I'm in such a hurry." We naturally blame another person's personality for their behavior, but blame situations for ours.

There's a corollary too: if a person gives you a strong indication of their personality, then you'll expect certain behavior from them. A famous experiment from the 1970s (since repeated in many variations) showed that this expectation is frequently wrong too.

Two psychologists at Princeton, John M. Darley and C. Daniel Batson, set out to understand what was more important for predicting behavior, people's inherent dispositions—what they had on their mind—or the situations they found themselves in.[2] The subjects were seminary students studying to become pastors. Darley and Batson told the subjects that they were studying religious education. While sitting in one building, they all filled out questionnaires designed to reveal personality traits, and then were told to go to another building. The reasons they were given to go were varied, and so was the degree of urgency. One group was told that they were to go to the other building to learn about jobs. A second group was told that they were to go to prepare a practice sermon on the subject of the Good Samaritan. Some were told that they were late for this next task and should rush over, while another group was told that they had finished early and had a little time, but that they should head over anyway.

Meanwhile, the psychologists positioned an actor slumped over on the path between the two buildings. The actor was directed to moan and cough. The real test was to see who would stop to help. Result? Whether the seminarians were going to the next building for a job or were thinking about writing a sermon on the Good Samaritan didn't make any difference in regard to how many stopped to help. Although it was thought that a group of seminarians studying to become pastors would be biased toward being helpful people, the questionnaire answers also failed to show any correlation between personality and stopping to help.

What did make a difference was urgency. Of the seminarians who were told they had time to spare, 63 percent stopped to help. Of the ones told they were in a hurry, only 10 percent stopped.

Being in a rush isn't an inherent disposition; it's a situation. Being a seminarian sounds like something inherent, but in fact it's also a situation. As a group, are seminarians predisposed to be helpful? And if so, is it because those are inherent qualities of their characters or because the situation of being a seminarian provokes behaviors associated with those words? The

Darley–Batson experiment shows, at least, that the situation of being a seminarian in a rush leads to different behaviors than being a seminarian at leisure.

This isn't to say people don't have personalities. Research does not disprove our common views about character, personality, and disposition. People do have all sorts of traits that persist over time or even throughout their lives. And people who are close to each other and of long acquaintance do get better at predicting each other's behavior in new situations. Nevertheless, inferring personality from a given behavior and predicting behavior based on personality (imagined or real) are both substantially less accurate than focusing on the situations people are in.[3]

For innovators, all this research indicates that it's problematic to rely on customer types. If you imagine that your customer is, for example, a young mother or a Gen X homeowner or a doctor, be aware that the type you're thinking of is probably less predictive of how they'll behave than the situation they find themselves in. Rather than thinking about a doctor, work out the details of a specific doctoring situation; you're more likely to find clues to their behavior by looking at their situation.

Confirmation Bias

Confirmation bias is the best known and best studied of any of the biases. The phrase covers lots of ways people hold on to their viewpoints and fail to examine them in a new light. It's related to the curse of knowledge, but covers other behaviors as well. For innovators, being able to examine and change viewpoints is paramount. Without that ability, your innovations will almost certainly rest on unexamined assumptions that are likely to be mistaken. Knowing how confirmation bias manifests itself is a step toward setting up procedures to overcome it.

Raymond Nickerson's classic review of the research around confirmation bias starts by laying out how pervasive and serious the problem really is: "If one were to attempt to identify a single problematic aspect of human reasoning that deserves attention above all others, the confirmation bias would have to be among the candidates for consideration. . . . One is led to wonder whether the bias, by itself, might account for a significant fraction of the disputes, altercations, and misunderstandings that occur among individuals, groups, and nations."[4]

In a courtroom, you'd expect each lawyer to lay out the best possible case for their client and try hard to poke holes in the opposition's case. We don't notice ourselves playing the part of lawyer for our own ideas and assumptions, but that's what we do. Sometimes that kind of behavior can be chalked up to motivated reasoning. If there's a dispute about who gets to keep some money, you or someone else, you'll be motivated to believe the arguments that support you as the rightful owner. More mysteriously, people build cases even when they aren't motivated in one direction or another; logical reasoning gets infected with confirmation bias even without any preexisting preferences.

Here are some of the biggest ways confirmation bias operates:

- Restricting attention to a favorite idea or view, not even noticing that there's a different way to see things

- Only looking for or noticing evidence that supports your view

- When you do see evidence that contradicts your belief, dismissing it or underweighting it compared to supportive evidence

- If you can't ignore contradictory evidence, adjusting your theory as little as possible to keep believing in the main parts of it

- Starting with a set of categories, such that the things you notice will magically fit within them

- Pure laziness—just gathering enough information to make sense of something and stopping there (without worrying about whether there might be a better explanation)

The curse of knowledge figures largely in all this. Knowing something, and being overconfident about what you think you know, feed into confirmation bias in the ways Nickerson catalogued.

Once you start noticing founders going around trying to confirm their preconceptions, you'll see confirmation bias everywhere. One entrepreneur we worked with (ironically enough, a psychologist) interviewed a series of prospective customers and asked them if they'd like to save money. Unsurprisingly, he received an overwhelmingly positive response. Another one excitedly related that he'd given a talk about his ideas to an audience of about a hundred people, and eleven of them came up afterward to tell him how much they loved his ideas. He never thought to follow up with the other eighty-nine. It's nearly impossible to find innovators who haven't misled themselves down some confirmation bias pathway.

CHAPTER 9
Decontaminating the Innovation Lab

While we were developing our understanding of the biases and cognitive illusions that posed problems for innovators, we were also working on creating an environment for taming them. We wanted to create a place where people interested in innovation could both learn specific things about innovation directly and also absorb and become part of a culture of competent innovation.

Becoming a Competent Innovator

In every organization, people learn how to use tools and follow explicit procedures. They also absorb the organizational culture and learn how to behave as members of that organization. These mindsets and habits percolate into who they are in work situations. One of our key goals at Flashpoint was to create a culture where people behaved as competent innovators. Flashpoint wasn't just intended as a place where startup founders could work and develop their businesses. It wasn't only a place for learning about ideas such as authentic demand and about psychological obstacles to innovation. Beyond those things, we wanted to create a community of

practice—a place where people could become competent innovators. Competence by itself isn't enough. Innovation isn't a paint-by-
numbers process—creativity, insight, and luck are always factors.
But competence beats incompetence.

Being competent at innovating goes back to the idea of being
stuck. Paul Simon got stuck writing "Bridge over Troubled Water,"
but he got himself unstuck and ended up with a classic. Competent
innovators get stuck, but they can tell that they're stuck early on, and
they can back out of the ditch and find a way forward. They do that
by finding and keeping their attention on worthwhile goals (nonindifference, not nots, and authentic demand) by avoiding traps such
as the curse of knowledge and fundamental attribution bias, and by
knowing and using the best tools available.

Collaboration is enormously valuable for becoming a competent
innovator. Community is crucially important for innovators, particularly because multiple perspectives are important for managing and
reducing biases and illusions, and for overcoming blind spots.

The romantic notion of a lone-wolf genius who comes up with
a great idea and makes it happen, like Howard Roark in Ayn Rand's
The Fountainhead, is not yet dead. Such people do exist, but for each
one who succeeds, dozens of similar people fail, and the ones who
do succeed usually fail on their next project. Competent innovators learn from and frequently work in community, because that's
what's most effective. Their batting average is higher.

Flashpoint did succeed in building a culture. It was housed in
a loft space on campus at Georgia Tech. For some reason, one of
the walls was painted a bright, shocking lime green, and companies

from each cohort would affix their logo to that wall before they left. One day Matt was visiting a company that had come through one of the earlier cohorts, in its own digs a few miles away. About twenty-five people were working away at screens in an open space, and one wall was painted that same lime green. Matt asked about it, and the CEO told him that three other former Flashpoint companies had done the same thing, painting one wall that color; these companies had been at Flashpoint for only four months, but their founders brought a token of its culture with them.

The Flashpoint culture was built around a set of ideas and practices, a cadence of work, and a set of tools. We (Merrick, Matt, and our colleagues) developed the culture and practices at Flashpoint specifically with a focus on formative innovation, which was appropriate for the startups we worked with. As large companies began joining Flashpoint cohorts, we discovered that many of these practices were also helpful in supporting the informative and transformative innovation needs of large established enterprises. The Principles and Practices section here reflects Flashpoint's main focus on startups. The subsequent section, Building an Innovative Environment at IBM, discusses some of Danny's work to create a similar culture within the larger IBM situation.

Principles and Practices

Unconditional Positive Regard

At Flashpoint we expected everyone in the practice to hold others in unconditional positive regard. This stance, borrowed from the psychologist Carl Rogers, involves showing complete support and acceptance of a person no matter what that person says. The psychological obstacles to innovating aren't personal failures; they're simply part of the way human minds work. We can no more make these distortions go away than we can change what people see with their eyes. So people making these errors don't deserve any less respect. Being wrong doesn't mean being bad or inferior; it's just that we're all capable of being less wrong.

Moreover, the ways that people are wrong are often clues that can help unlock nonindifferences. Over time, we came to see unconditional positive regard as a cornerstone of innovation. It not only eases tensions and facilitates frank conversations but also acts as a bulwark against some of the misunderstandings that can come via the curse of knowledge and other cognitive illusions.

Radical Candor

A lot of the work of Deliberate Innovation is to notice one another's blind spots. And when someone calls out your blind spots, you're liable to feel blindsided. It's easy to feel like a fool. In polite society, making people feel like fools is discouraged, but innovation cultures can't afford that sort of politeness. So the work requires radical candor. The phrase was popularized as a management idea developed by Kim Scott in her book of the same name.[1] The book provides advice for managing teams, but innovation projects are not like most business projects, where the goal is to reach a known objective quickly or under budget. So radical candor in innovation isn't so much about guiding and incentivizing team members. Instead, it's about creating a space where people can say what they're thinking straightforwardly, secure in knowing that they will be heard respectfully and that their words won't be taken as a personal affront.

Without unconditional positive regard, radical candor easily devolves into accusations or just makes people uncomfortable, so they clam up. But with positive regard as a foundation, radical candor can elevate team discussions to a level of much greater clarity. The experience is difficult, but can be exhilarating. No one's ideas are treated with kid gloves. On the contrary, nearly everyone at Flashpoint experienced being blindsided, having their ideas and beliefs undercut or rejected, feeling foolish. We worked hard to make this kind of communication tolerable, on the basis that we were all in it together. None of us notice that we're not noticing things; none of us are immune to biases and cognitive illusions. It's a favor—a gift, really—to tap someone on the shoulder and in effect tell them, "You may be falling into an error here in the way you're approaching this . . ." or "I've noticed that you seem to be confirming a bias here." Even so, it's a gift that's not usually appreciated when it arrives. The people who helped run Flashpoint often felt as though they needed to act as therapists. One great innovation, instituted by a cohort member, was "Flash Pint"—a trip for cohort members to a nearby bar after a particularly tough day on the schedule.

Cadence

Innovation is essentially unlike other business practices in that the end goal can't be scoped out in advance. Deliberate innovators know the *type* of their goal. They know it's an unmet authentic demand around which they can build a business. But they don't know specifically what it is. How do you measure progress toward a goal if you can't identify it until you've arrived?

Just like any other team project, innovation projects need measurements and milestones or they risk foundering. Where projects are aimed at known goals, they can be broken down into measurable components. Innovation projects, especially those involving formative innovation, don't work that way.

At Flashpoint, Merrick used an analogy from aviation: ground speed versus airspeed. With formative innovation, the specific authentic demand you're looking for can't, by definition, be known in advance. So instead of measuring proximity to that goal, metrics are designed to measure activities that move you faster in the right direction. This is something like airspeed, which measures the activity of the airplane even if wind or other factors make it impossible to translate that activity directly to distance covered on the ground.

For deliberate innovators, maintaining airspeed requires maintaining a work cadence. Flashpoint put founders into a regular cadence of weekly activities that increased their "airspeed" and thereby raised the probability of reaching their destination. Teams planned their weekly activities, got support in structuring them, and in five-minute presentations every Tuesday night showed everyone what they'd done. The presentations were followed by a group dinner, which helped knit back together the frayed nerves of the presenters. Wednesday mornings were for weekly kickoff sessions where teams debriefed about their presentations and structured activities for the next week. Other aspects of the cadence had longer cycles. Early weeks focused more on learning both about issues such as confirmation bias and fundamental attribution bias, and about using the core Flashpoint tools—situation diagrams and DPIs (see chapters 10 and 11). As the weeks progressed, there were fewer learning sessions and higher expectations about using the tools.

Paying Attention to Indifference

If you're an innovator bent on building something that will matter to people and that they will accept into their lives, there's nothing worse than indifference. What could be worse than pitching your pet idea and then watching your audience wander away, not even disliking your idea, but just not caring about it and letting it drift out of their minds? That makes indifference hard to see, in two different ways. It's difficult emotionally when you see it. And it easily avoids notice, because we're strongly motivated to confirm our positive preconceptions.

But when you pay enough attention, you'll see indifference everywhere, and especially with respect to your innovative ideas. Always remember, the things that people are nonindifferent to are things they cope with, that they get a grip on. Whenever there's a not not, there's probably a situation that people have built so that the not not will not be violated. Unmet authentic demand crops up when situations change that they're not equipped to cope with. A characteristic of stable situations is that the people involved are skillfully coping with their authentic demands in some way so that they don't appear as demands. When an innovator sees indifference and mistakes it for nonindifference, it's like reading a sign backwards and driving in the wrong direction. At Flashpoint we always tried to remind people to overcome their reluctance to notice indifference.

Attending to Process

Is your idea for a business or for a product a good idea or a bad idea? A central tenet at Flashpoint was that we didn't know. We do know that the biases and psychological obstacles that everyone suffers from make it extraordinarily hard for an innovator to discern the strengths and weaknesses of their ideas. The best we can do is to make sure that the way you came to the idea was sound.

The "inner loop" of the Deliberate Innovation process, the way founders worked to discover unmet authentic demands they could build businesses around, used DPIs and situation diagrams. This process will be described in detail in the next two chapters. Flashpoint's culture supported that inner loop by downplaying outcomes and rewarding attention to process.

Odysseus Bargains

Odysseus bargains are named after an incident in the adventures of the ancient Greek hero of Homer's *Odyssey*. Odysseus was sailing past the island of the Sirens, supernatural women who with their beautiful, seductive songs lured sailors to approach and shipwreck themselves on the rocks. Odysseus wanted to hear their songs but also to remain safe. He filled the ears of his crew with wax and had them tie him to the mast, with orders to ignore anything he might say. Hearing the Sirens, he begged his men to free him and steer toward the rocks, but they ignored him and were able to sail by safely.

At Flashpoint, we used all sorts of Odysseus bargains to protect ourselves from biases and cognitive illusions. It started with our application process. The goal of debiasing our application process was to make the best selections possible. That meant choosing to admit startups that we were most likely to be able to help and that were most likely to succeed. But debiasing our process had the additional effect of debiasing in the common racial sense of the word.

Most startup accelerators and innovation teams of all types are overwhelmingly populated by white men. The exceptions tend to be programs specifically designed for women or minorities. Instead of making that sort of exception, we debiased the acceptance process. We stopped looking at videos from candidates. We had names and gender pronouns stripped out of applications before judges saw them, so they wouldn't be biased by assumptions about gender or race. We had the judges score candidates based only on the criteria we believed mattered. We had multiple judges score each applicant, and if the different scores weren't correlated, we didn't use them. We didn't let the judges watch video of candidates, again, to avoid bias. Finally, scores were added up and applicants were ranked. Everyone who rated above a threshold was essentially accepted; only then did we interview the applicants to confirm details of the application and to describe and pitch our program. The result of this debiasing effort was a series of cohorts in which women and minorities usually made up 50 to 70 percent of the people in the room.

When applicants were selected and the program began, we continued using Odysseus bargains to protect ourselves from biases. For the first months of the program, Merrick and Matt would refuse to listen to any product ideas. They knew that any immediate judgments they made on the basis of the ideas would be biased and would color subsequent discussion. Founders normally came into the program with product ideas they were eager to share. It was a constant struggle to avoid talking and making judgments about initial product ideas. But we knew that the process was more important, and our judgments about product ideas and value propositions wouldn't be useful.

Common Language

Terms and phrases such as *not not, authentic demand, DPI, I've noticed that. . ., mud pie*, and so on were defined in practice and used as shorthand in ongoing conversations. Most of these concepts and terms are quite different from those commonly used by innovators outside Flashpoint. They served to reinforce the ideas, facilitate communication, and bring together the community.

Building an Innovative Environment at IBM

With Flashpoint, Merrick had taken a stand and carved out from Georgia Tech the freedom to build the best environment for innovation he could. Most innovators in large enterprises have their own sets of constraints. They have to contend with existing cultures, pressure for quarterly results, and bosses who might or might not be supportive.

At IBM, Danny didn't have Flashpoint's tools or language or focus on biases and cognitive illusions. As described in chapter 3, he and his colleagues did find their way to solving the transformational challenges that led to WebSphere, but they did it by trial and error. In the process, they had to fight and win battles that a different environment and a common language might have enabled them to avoid.

Nevertheless, over time Danny did build a space for better innovation in IBM's software businesses. When Matt discussed this topic with Danny, it appeared that Danny had managed to intuitively use some of the same principles we had at Flashpoint. To wit, encouraging candor but grounding it in respect and regard for conflicting ideas. There was also a version of an Odysseus bargain, to encourage people to raise issues that others needed to hear but didn't necessarily want to.

Danny introduced these techniques in order to cope with both specific challenges and an overriding general challenge. The specific challenges were that he was running a global business, selling various software products in dozens of countries around the world. Each situation was different, so the demand for the products themselves, and for the way they were sold, varied in ways that weren't obvious from IBM's headquarters in New York. A best seller in France might have a weak market in Germany and no market at all in Hong Kong. Danny needed to understand what was going on.

The overriding general challenge was to build a sustainable, growing business. The antagonist to sustainability was the perennial issue of short-term, quarterly returns. Investments in long-term growth threatened to divert people or resources away from meeting this quarter's numbers.

Danny worked at opening up space for innovation by pushing in three directions: with his bosses, with his customers, and with his teams.

Bosses. Danny worked to make his bosses comfortable with what he was doing. Instead of cutting them out and trying to build his own fiefdom, he cut them in on important decisions. He listened and always took into account what they had to say, without necessarily agreeing or following instructions. He reminded himself that they might know things he didn't know, or have agendas for the company as a whole that might supersede his agenda. Danny argued for a commitment to sustainable growth and backed up the arguments with his own personal commitment. The instances when he took his bosses to task and was openly critical stand out to him as milestones in his career. He was able to do that because in his mind he had the job—the job never had him. If push came to shove, he could find another job elsewhere. Nevertheless, developing a relationship of mutual respect and support took years of sustained effort.

Customers. Danny racked up more frequent-flier miles than many at IBM, and he did it in order to visit and talk with customers. Although he wasn't an expert on confirmation bias, the curse of knowledge, and so on, he had a feel for the problems of motivated reasoning. No one is more motivated than a salesperson, so Danny knew he couldn't rely on them alone for an understanding of what was going on with customers. His constant customer meetings were rarely sales calls. Instead, he cultivated standing apart from the sales process, as someone who was seeking understanding or acting as an honest broker between IBM and the customer. Selling IBM products was almost never at the forefront of these conversations.

Team. Danny needed the people who worked for him to be as honest and forthright as possible about what they heard and noticed. Honest and forthright doesn't mean gentle. Mark once watched him chew out his team, and remembers wanting to crawl under the table, even though he wasn't directly involved. But the reason for Danny's anger was that he hadn't been told about something. People who worked for Danny quickly learned that if they didn't tell him the truth, they could get in real trouble. But if they failed at some task or something hadn't gone right and they were open about it, they could expect a very different reaction— good advice, and support for making things right. In a culture where too many leaders had a "shoot the messenger" mentality, Danny carved out a space for openness.

Danny wasn't familiar with Merrick's unconditional positive regard approach, but he understood that candor and respect were two sides of a coin and that it was self-defeating to try to build a culture of candor without respect.

He had known bosses who demanded candor from their teams, but both punished people who were open about their shortcomings and reacted badly to criticism. Instead, Danny talked to his teams about his shortcomings at IBM and said things people at the company might be hesitant to say, as a way of signaling that it was OK to be honest and open.

Unconditional positive regard, candor, and the more specific elements of culture that Merrick introduced at Flashpoint are all aimed at creating a culture that fosters innovation. Ideally, they create something like a well-prepared garden, with the right water and soil and sun and shade for innovation to grow. But gardeners also need to plant and tend their plants; likewise, deliberate innovators need to come up with and develop their innovations. At Flashpoint the concrete process for this was a cycle of creating and improving a customer model that centered around what we called a situation diagram.

CHAPTER 10
Diagramming Situations to Uncover Authentic Demand

Sometime around 1534, Andreas Vesalius took a hanged man down from a gibbet in Paris and examined the body carefully. That was a seminal moment in his investigations into how the human body is put together, and it helped launch Vesalius as the father of modern anatomy. A few centuries later in Lausanne, Alexander Osterwalder wrote a seminal PhD thesis called "The Business Model Ontology," in which he set out to do something similar: pin down the anatomy not of a person but of a business.[1] That thesis was the beginning of a journey that led Merrick to create situation diagrams, a key tool that we employed at Flashpoint.

Getting to Situation Diagrams

Osterwalder's goal was "to provide an ontology that makes it possible to explicate a firm's business model. In other words, the proposed artifact helps a firm to formally describe its value proposition, its customers, the relationship with them, the necessary intra- and inter-firm infrastructure, and its profit model."[2]

The visualization of Osterwalder's results is called the business model canvas (BMC). It purports to show the essential parts of every business. Just as in anatomy, where the details of how animals are put together vary enormously but all animals share essential systems for eating, sensing, moving, and reproducing, so similar elements can be identified in businesses. According to the model, every business from a corner store to Exxon Mobil will include these "organs":

- A value proposition
- A way of creating that value, including activities, partners, and resources
- A way of harvesting that value, including customers, channels to them, and relationships with them
- A financial model—for a business to be sustainable, the cost of creating the value must be lower, in the long run, than the value harvested from it

Thanks to Osterwalder's collaborator Steve Blank and then others, the BMC (figure 10.1) is now a common sight at business accelerators and on the desks of entrepreneurs. Founders have come to use the canvas as a template for their startups. The idea is that if you iterate on and ultimately validate the parts that fit into each box, you will end up with a template for a business that, once it's executed correctly, will be viable.

The BMC was becoming a common tool during the rocky start of Damballa when Merrick was trying to understand why

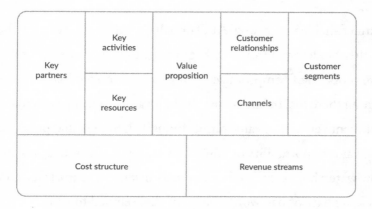

Figure 10.1. Business model canvas

Source: Created by Business Model Foundry AG, Copyright 2020. Material available under Public License at https://commons.wikimedia.org/wiki/File:Business_Model_Canvass_template.png.[3]

value propositions weren't working as expected. Grappling with this problem and watching how founders were using the BMC, Merrick kept circling back to two questions:

- What should we really be modeling?

- What role does the value proposition actually play?

Osterwalder derived the BMC by analyzing existing, established businesses, and that's what it was meant to describe. It seemed obvious that if you wanted to create a business, you could use the BMC as a blueprint—your business would ultimately have to fit the model, so why not build from it? But what if the obvious was wrong? The goal of the innovator, after all, is to do something that fits into the life of the people they're innovating for. Prior to accomplishing that, we have all these assumptions about value propositions. At Humminbird, Jim thought he knew from the beginning how to fit in: by helping fishermen catch fish. He was wrong. At Damballa, we thought we knew the authentic demand from the beginning: to help customers solve the problem of compromised computers. It looked like we were wrong there too. In both cases, the innovators came up with many different versions of value propositions: fish finders that provided the value of portability or of waterproofing or of working in shallow water; bot detectors that stopped click fraud or trust fraud, or stealing data or passwords. None of that seemed to work.

So maybe the first problem for an innovator to solve isn't how to create a business that looks like a business but rather to discern the unmet authentic demand one could build around. To fix that problem, *the model that requires iteration and validation isn't a model of the business, it is a model of the customer.*

Drawing on research on the effect of situations on behavior discussed in chapter 8, Merrick began thinking that the thing to be modeled was the customer's situation, because that's the situation that most reliably predicts their behavior. So instead of trying to model the customer or client in terms of their demographics or personalities or even their problems, he decided to try modeling the situations they were part of.

People, of course, are in countless different situations, both simultaneously and over the course of their lives. They are in parenting situations, sibling situations, work situations; they're in situations as vegetarians, Dodgers fans, and on and on. Trying to diagram the whole thing would be impossible. But maybe it was possible to diagram the fraction of situations that could connect to the innovator and the situation *they* were in.

One component of nearly all situations people are in is the stuff they use to cope with that situation. Dodgers fans use tickets and box scores; vegetarians use cookbooks and vegetarian restaurants; parents use diapers and school buses. From the point of view of a company interested in providing tickets or cookbooks or diapers, it isn't necessary to model the person's situation in a holistic way. The innovator can get what they need by modeling the customer's situation with respect to the stuff they use that matters to the innovator. An innovator at a company that makes diapers probably doesn't have to model their customer's situation with respect to sports tickets, just as a ticket company doesn't need to worry about diapers.

The second question Merrick asked was, What role does the value proposition actually play? He didn't know it, but over at IBM, Danny was grappling with the same problem. His marketing department could fluently describe the value propositions driving their products. But the descriptions never stuck. A product might be offered with the value proposition that it was cheaper than competing items. Customers would tell the salespeople that they bought it because it was cheaper, and managers felt that the value proposition had been confirmed. Marketers and salespeople thought they understood what was going on, until customers began buying a more expensive product, and they had to start again from scratch. Sometimes these value propositions seemed to label something real, and sometimes they didn't, and sometimes they worked for a while and then stopped working. Altogether, the whole idea of a value proposition was too slippery to depend on. Merrick and Danny were looking at the same issue, but while Danny was trying to manage it, Merrick was trying to build a theory for it.

He noticed that in the Osterwalder BMC, the value proposition took center stage because it held everything together. Services and products were created to offer the value; clients and customers made purchases because the proposition offered value. The pieces of the BMC stuck together because the value proposition acted like glue.

But if one looks at customer situations as situations, no glue is necessary. Situations are what they are because they hold themselves together through a web of interlocking not nots. As long as a situation remains, it's stable because the pieces are like a jigsaw puzzle, holding on to each other.

With these thoughts in mind, Merrick made several changes to the BMC. First, he refocused it on the customer who might buy, instead of the company that might sell. Second, he looked at the customer's situation, not their demographics or problems. Third, he took the value proposition box out altogether. Finally, he simplified, narrowing the diagram down to just four boxes: actions, relationships, equipment, and channels, as shown in table 10.1.

The four boxes are for the four parts of a situation that an observer can see and test:

1. Actions: people doing things

2. Equipment/Resources: products and services used in the performance of actions

3. Relationships: activities by people other than the person whose actions we're looking at, serving as a resource for those actions

4. Channels: pathways by which equipment or other people's actions reach and impact the situation

Actions

This box refers to a person of interest's actions or behaviors of interest. It might be something like signing an invoice or stopping in front of a display window or making a phone call.

Equipment/Resources

In the modern world, people usually cope with the help of tools or, more broadly, equipment. The idea of equipment doesn't just include actual tools or machinery. It encompasses services and anything with which a person in a situation copes and maintains a grip. Situations

Table 10.1. Situation diagram

Actions	Relationships
Equipment/Resources	Channels

shape equipment and equipment shapes situations. Take an elevator. A great elevator situated in a small apartment building may be a terrible elevator in a commercial high-rise. What's less obvious is that the elevator technology also impacts the ways people using the elevator cope. Earlier-generation elevators required operators to open and close the door and navigate to the correct floor. When a new generation of automatic push-button elevators became common, many people still demanded operators. Today elevators without buttons, operated by cards matched to specific floors, are again disturbing and interacting with the way people perceive and interact with elevators.

Thus solid, unchanging, physical equipment is nevertheless very changeable depending on the situation. The same cell phone that may be a lifeline for the child stuck at school can be an instrument for holding a meeting, a SKU for meeting a sales quota at Apple, or a travel facilitator, translator, bird identifier, flashlight, alarm clock, and so on. What the phone *is* is never simply describable by its features. The phone may always weigh thirty grams, but in one situation that could translate into "too heavy" and in another "not substantial enough." It's sometimes useful to characterize equipment as "resources."

Relationships

Relationships are a kind of resource. People can't cope without them, but coping with the help of relationships is contextual in a way that makes it quite different than simply using equipment. A customer is a resource. So are team members, bosses, support staff, fans, investors, friends, and anyone with whom an individual copes with their situation. Unlike with equipment, reciprocity is the key to relationships. A person coping with a situation is also a resource for those on the other side of the relationship.

Channels

A channel is the structure or path by which equipment or relationship resources are delivered in order to enable the action. Retail shelves, an app store, a subscription, a zoom call or meeting, a telephone, a text—all of these can be channels.

Diagramming the Lumping Business

Startup companies and new products are almost always launched prematurely, with a false start. But unlike with a footrace, no one blows a whistle and forces the company back into the blocks to start over. With startups and truly innovative products, this kind of false start is hard to detect. False starts are launched by ideas; real starts begin with uncovering an authentic demand. The company that became RoadSync is a good example of restarting around authentic demand.

One day, a tall Haitian named Akmann Van-Mary applied to Flashpoint. Akmann had worked in several different parts of the trucking industry; he owned and ran a third-party logistics company matching truckers with shippers. It was a solid business, but while he was at it he came up with an idea that looked to him like a golden, scalable opportunity. The problematic situation he had in mind occurred when truckers unloaded their trucks.[4]

When trucks show up at a warehouse or logistics center, the truckers need lumpers and warehouse managers to complete their business. Lumpers load and unload trucks; warehouse managers and their staff manage the flow of operations, direct the truckers into queues and dock slots, and get the goods documented and transferred to wherever they're going next.

Akmann knew these situations well, and he saw them breaking down all the time. Queues would move slowly and truckers were forced to bide their time, missing deadlines and burning fuel. A truck would be directed to a dock where it waited for lumpers to come and unload, but would then be shunted to the side to make way for another truck because the lumpers hadn't arrived. Akmann had an insight that the problem lay in the payment system. Payment in this business was a mess. It was all done with paper processing. Paying in cash was illegal under federal law, the legacy of a long history of scams and tax dodges. Lumping costs were purportedly included in the freight rates paid to drivers or trucking companies, but in practice, drivers often ended up paying extra lumping charges and not being reimbursed. Even though paying in cash was illegal, it was still widespread. Problems such as damaged items or warehouses that required shipments to be stacked differently gummed up the works.

The standard alternative to cash had been invented in the 1970s by a company called Comdata and was called Comchek. Truckers would arrive at warehouses with a bill of lading and a stack of Comchek blanks. A lumper would take the bill of lading and generate an invoice. The trucker would call a number, and in most cases reach an automated system or twenty-four-hour service that would take the information from the invoice and provide a fourteen-to-eighteen-digit code, which the trucker would write on a Comchek. They would hand the Comchek over to the lumper, who would make another call, receive a complementary code, and write that on the check, at which point the check became negotiable. A situation diagram from the point of view of a trucker might look like table 10.2.

The four parts of the situation diagram gave Akmann a way to think more clearly, and explicitly, about what comes together to make that a particular moment. Diagramming is a tool for thinking, not a solution. Diagramming situations isn't innovating; it's just writing down what you know already, or think you know, in a usable

Table 10.2. First situation diagram for RoadSync: Trucker

Actions	Relationships
Call shipper with invoice in hand and receive a multidigit code; write that on a blank Comchek	Lumper (who provides invoice) Shipper or intermediary (who provides code)
Equipment/Resources	**Channels**
Telephone Invoice (from lumper) Comchek blanks Code (from shipper) Bank that accepts Comcheks and works with this warehouse site	Phone to shipper Face-to-face on the dock

format. Situation diagrams uncover—and enable innovators to test—situations, or aspects of situations that the innovator already understands; they don't uncover what one doesn't already know.

Akmann felt that he was a good way toward a big new business. By replacing the outdated Comchek system with something modern and simple, he could make truckers' lives much easier; they'd flock to it. He didn't have a specific technology in mind, but new payment systems were coming up all over; why not one for truckers? That's what Akmann, with his experience and expertise in trucking and third-party logistics, imagined.

Deliberate Innovation, however, proceeds not by imagining a nerve but by touching a nerve. Merrick suggested that Akmann go down to a warehouse dock and try to get a trucker interested. When Akmann didn't go that week, Merrick suggested it again. And then the following week, and multiple times in between. Akmann's resistance to the suggestions was entirely typical. He's not a shy guy, and he felt comfortable in those environments; those weren't the issues. But Akmann had made a momentous decision. He had a comfortable business. He had a recognized place in the community and social life of an industry. But he'd decided to put all that at risk, to roll the dice, on the strength of an idea. That idea was Akmann's false start, the mythological takeoff point of a new business.

Startup founders and company executives don't like to research and double-check their starting points. They often pretend to do that—pitching the ideas, testing them in a way that's biased toward positive answers—but their hearts aren't in it. Once you've decided to stake so much on an idea, it's hard to avoid selling the idea, setting up questions to get confirmation, and refusing to hear contradictory information. Questioning and examining every aspect of an idea doesn't feel like a sober necessity; it feels like a threat. For about six weeks, Merrick and the Flashpoint team urged Akmann to go down to a loading dock and test this idea with the truckers. Finally, he overcame his reluctance and did it. The truckers didn't let him know whether they loved it or hated the idea; they were busy, and he couldn't get their attention.

Hearing this story for the first time, Danny nodded. "Of course," he said. "The same thing happened all the time at IBM. You'd see a problem that customers had, point it out to them, and propose a possible solution, and you couldn't get their attention. It wasn't that you were wrong about the problem, necessarily. It was more like the old saying 'When you're up to your ass in alligators, you don't think about draining the swamp.' A situation where potential customers might consider or buy a solution was entirely different from a situation where they were actually engaged in dealing with the problem. They were too busy coping to even listen."

Akmann didn't give up, though. The situation diagram helped set a course. In the Relationships quadrant of the diagram in table 10.2 there are lumpers, shippers, and intermediaries. He spoke to all of them. The indifferent reaction he'd gotten from truckers came up again from lumpers. He heard some complaining about the Comcheks, but nothing substantial. However, when talking with a shipper one day, he heard something unexpected. The shipper said, "I just wish I could sleep through the night." That was a new one.

They were talking about payment platforms and logistics issues, and the guy brought up a personal problem.

Akmann knew perfectly well that people talk all the time about all sorts of things, and most of it is just gossip. But still, if value is to be found, incongruous statements are a good place to look. Akmann asked why he said that, and the shipper explained that issuing Comchek validation codes was a headache. Truckers arrived at loading docks all over the country at all hours. There were often problems, such as a mistake on the bill of lading, or something that got broken in the lumping process, or goods that had gone bad in some way. When things went wrong, the shipper had to get on the phone and take care of the problem, wherever and whenever it occurred, or the shipment would not be delivered. That added up to a lot of sleepless nights.

It was time for another situation diagram (table 10.3) that relates the situation of the trucker to the situation of the shipper.

The action in the Shipper diagram links to the action in the Trucker diagram. Elements in both situation diagrams are the elements without which something will fail to happen. If the trucker doesn't deliver a Comchek with a code on it to the lumper, the load will not be unloaded. If the shipper doesn't deliver a code to the trucker, the trucker won't deliver that check. If the shipper doesn't have a contingency-code directory, they will not deliver a code over the phone to the trucker in a contingent case. The chain of actions spreads across many people performing actions via channels, and the actions, performed through the channels, clarify how the relationships function (along with the support of other relationships and resources or equipment).

Table 10.3. Situation diagram for RoadSync,
relating trucker situation (top) to shipper situation (bottom)

Actions

Call shipper with invoice in hand and receive a multidigit code; write that on a blank Comchek

Relationships

Lumper (who provides invoice and accepts payment)

Shipper or intermediary (who has a cash account and provides a payment code)

Equipment/Resources

Telephone

Invoice (from lumper)

Comchek blanks

Code (from shipper)

Channels

Phone to shipper

Face-to-face on the dock

Actions

Provide a payment validation code to a trucker trying to deliver a shipment

Relationships

Trucker

Comchek help-desk person

Equipment/Resources

Telephone

Invoice

Code-generating system

Contingency-code directory

Channels

Voice phone to trucker

Voice phone to Comchek

But now a strange phenomenon has appeared—*sleepless nights.* In this simplified version of situation diagramming, the reason that sleepless nights happen is already obvious. If a shipper ignores a phone call, the trucker won't get a code to put on a Comchek and a shipment won't be delivered. In order to continue being a shipper, they've got to answer that phone whenever the call comes in. But why did the shipper mention it? More exactly, what would go wrong if he didn't mention that to Akmann?

Probably nothing. This sort of strange phenomenon appears frequently, and mostly it doesn't amount to anything. But there's a potential authentic demand here. It's possible that if the shipper didn't mention his sleepless nights to Akmann, Akmann couldn't come up with a technology to help get him back to bed.

After lots of testing, the sleepless nights did turned out to be important. In further conversations, it came up again and again. One shipper said to Akmann, "Tell me where I can park $50,000 so you can use it to pay the truckers." The shippers were looking for ways to help Akmann help them. He was on to something.

Akmann knew and cared about the trucking industry in general; he started the company with an idea about helping truckers pay lumpers more efficiently. By testing and diagramming, he found something else: authentic demand among shippers. He had been in the right ballpark, but he couldn't see the ball; it wasn't where he had expected to find it. But he had uncovered a small, reliable secret. It wasn't that truckers would find value in a more efficient payment system; it was that shippers would pay for something that enabled them to sleep through the night. That was the kernel of authentic demand that was like a real starting gun. The company wasn't out of the woods, but now, just like Humminbird's Jim Balkcom and his insight about recreational fishermen, Akmann had a compass; he could start figuring out how to get out of the woods. From there, it wasn't 100 percent smooth sailing, but RoadSync now had a direction. The company was recently valued at $230 million.

From Situation Diagrams to Authentic Demand

Diagramming situations clarifies how authentic demand arises from within them and how the components of those situations stick together. People in situations cope with them so that the situation remains in place; when gaps open, they act to fill them. So, for example, when a person is a student, they may maintain their grip on being a student by engaging in activities such as attending classes, and they may have a piece of equipment such as a schedule that lets them know the time and place of each class. To maintain a grip on the situation, the student will be nonindifferent to that schedule. If it's on a piece of paper and they lose it, a gap will have opened up, and they'll search high and low for it. The authentic demand is for the gap to be closed and the situation maintained, but it's expressed by the customer as demand for the object, the piece of paper.

For an innovator, an object like a paper schedule, or any other equipment (product or service) is not what's in demand. The demand is for the gap closing that's accomplished through that object in a particular situation. It's convenient but misleading to think of the demand as demand for the object; more precisely, it's demand via the object for the gap closing. Thinking of the demand as being for the object itself obscures both the size of the market and the risk that the gap may be closed in some other way that wouldn't be noticed as competitive until it's too late.

This is a commonplace in marketing. The adage "customers don't buy a quarter-inch drill bit; they buy a quarter-inch hole" is attributed to Theodore Levitt, but versions of the saying go back at least a century. The idea of selling solutions rather than products is ubiquitous. These kinds of truisms go far enough to be useful reminders for marketers and salespeople. But innovators work upstream from marketers and salespeople, in the sense that marketing and sales pitches revolve around an authentic demand that the seller already thinks is valid. Uncovering an unmet authentic demand, and uncovering and addressing the counterforces that hold people back from closing that gap themselves, take place prior to that. These are the name of the innovation game.

Using the Diagrams

The analytical way to think of situation diagrams is that they are forms designed for accurate situational bookkeeping. We all make sense of situations. The "sense" of a situation involves (often unconsciously) explaining to ourselves how the situation "works." There's normally something happening, people involved, some equipment, and some way (channel through which) various actions take place. We frequently insert a "why" into this sensemaking, intuitively thinking, "That driver cut me off because he's a jerk" or "That person bought that shirt to save money." Taking the value proposition box out of a situation diagram is like taking the "why" out of an informal sensemaking process. The format leads an innovator toward making sense in terms of "what" and "how," without recourse to "why."

The diagrams are a key part of Deliberate Innovation; they are like home base in an ongoing loop of activity—noticing, raising questions, revising how to see things, and, with that new way of seeing, noticing more. As evidence accrues, deliberate innovators adjust the diagrams to take it into account, until they can't disprove or further adjust the explanation. Situation diagrams never reach the point of completely comprehending a situation; we never know precisely what's taking place with human beings and can't predict any action with 100 percent accuracy. But mature situation diagrams are more reliable than other ways of understanding and predicting the behavior of potential customers.

The emotional way to think of situation diagrams is that they are maps of suffering. People are always acting to get or keep a grip on situations, which means that they are always failing to get or losing their grip. The feeling involved is always some sort of pain. The diagrams show where the pain lies, because the net of not nots inevitably involves attempts to get a grip in some way that conflict with getting or maintaining a grip on something else, or reveal circumstances that can't be coped with.

This emotional perspective on the diagrams is important because it opens up the question of the innovator's role. Why does an innovator innovate? An inventor can be an inventor just by tinkering. But an innovator can only innovate deliberately by caring. They have to match their caring to what the customer, underneath it all, cares about. The word *care* has two meanings: to attend to, and to care for. Innovation straddles both meanings. Innovators attend to the potential customer's situation in order to understand the not nots and notice the nonindifferences. Innovators care about the customer's situation because they're moved to alleviate the suffering found in the situation.

CHAPTER 11
Uncovering Authentic Demand with DPIs

When Merrick suggested that Akmann head down to a load-ing dock and try to get some attention, Akmann balked. It took weeks of persistent nudging to get him to do it. In the previous chapter, we talked about his psychological resistance. When you've already decided to take a big risk and start a company or launch a new product or project, why take the additional big risk of finding out that your idea is no good? Sure, that "eyes wide shut" approach is irrational. But the curse of knowledge, confirmation bias, and other cognitive illusions were there to help Akmann rationalize it. You can avoid asking, assuming you already know the answers, as Akmann did at first. Or you can ask questions that will only get positive response ("Excuse me sir—how would you feel about a product that could save you a lot of money?") Or you could only listen for the confirmations and dismiss the disconfirmations as special, limited cases. There are lots of ways to not learn anything.

At Flashpoint we developed an approach calculated to manage those pitfalls as much as possible, called Documented

Primary Interactions, or DPIs for short. A DPI is an interaction between a prospective innovator and a potential customer (or sometimes with another potential stakeholder, such as a supplier or investor or employee). DPIs must

- Be documented, so that they can be planned, assessed, and remembered consistently. Documentation includes documenting the design of the DPI as an experiment beforehand and recording what actually happens, preferably by audio or video recording, but if not, through notes written right afterward. It also includes any necessary logging or tagging that will make the DPI accessible later on.

- Be conducted with people involved in the situation at hand, as distinct from experts or other outsiders opining about a situation they aren't directly party to. Primaries are people who are actually in situations. Secondaries are people talking about how other people they know or work with operate. Tertiaries are research reports or survey results. DPIs focus only on primaries.

- Be constructed as an interaction intended to bring out a response that will provide information about a nonindifference. This often involves doing or saying something that breaches a norm, in order to test whether or not the person is indifferent to the change.

A DPI is one interaction in a Deliberate Innovation process that usually involves 200–400 separate such interactions, usually over a three-to-six-month period. As illustrated in figure 11.1, the results of DPIs feed into situation diagrams, leading to adjusting the diagrams and figuring out the next thing to explore through more DPIs.

DPIs serve three tightly connected functions. The first is to provide content for situation diagrams. It is important to recognize and embrace the fact that most behavior is determined not by forethought and analysis but by the indifference and nonindifferences that exist in the situations. Accordingly, DPIs aren't for figuring out how a person analyzes their situation but for unearthing and stress-testing the innovator's view of a situation's

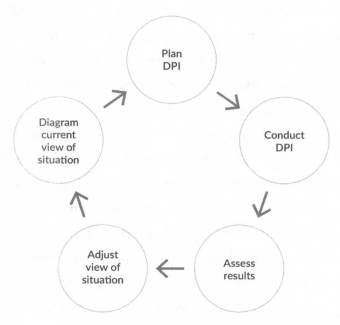

Figure 11.1. The DPI cycle

143

indifferences and nonindifferences, leading to the construction of a reliable situation diagram. An example of a distinction might be that a guy on a fishing boat may be indifferent to wearing a sweater or a fleece jacket, but he's likely to be nonindifferent to putting on a tuxedo or going naked.

Putting together the structure of a situation includes seeing how equipment fits. People cope with their situations with the help of equipment, but if the innovator doesn't see the situation as it is, the function of equipment can easily be misconstrued. The affordances and limitations of any equipment are bound up in the situation (remember: they're mud pie).

The second function of DPIs is to learn how to become a meaningful part of the customer's situations. In the beginning, the innovator and their innovation are outside the situation and are matters of indifference to the people in them. Becoming part of the situation is a process of becoming of value in given situations.

The third and maybe the most important function of DPIs is to support the innovator in changing themselves and their own organizations to become a meaningful part of the customer's situations. In the beginning, regardless of whatever bold ideas, cool technologies, experience, and confidence they might have, the innovator and their innovation are outside the situation and are matters of indifference to the people inside. DPIs are at the center of a process of personal and organizational change, a process of transforming from someone and something that isn't part of the system in question into someone or something that that is.

People at the Center for Deliberate Innovation developed detailed, step-by-step instructions for conducting DPIs. An edited version of their work is included here as an appendix. But DPIs are most clearly understood in process. The story of Mary Lynn Realff using DPIs imparts a better sense of the process than any description.

Caring about Team Dynamics

Along with the cohorts of business people who went through Flashpoint, Georgia Tech's Center for Deliberate Innovation has hosted university cohorts, and Mary Lynn was a member of one of these. They have been made up of professors and professional staff aiming to innovate in academia. Mary Lynn's experience is a case study in using DPIs to uncover authentic demand.[1]

Mary Lynn is an engineering professor and associate chair of her department at a large research university, with expertise in materials science. Team dynamics and effective collaboration are not her field, but today she's in high demand as an expert and trainer on that subject. Professors in the engineering department and all over the university and in other universities call frequently, asking for her help or the help of assistants she's trained. Two companies have reached out to her to pitch building a product from her methods. This wasn't always the case.

Five years ago, as Mary Lynn taught her engineering classes, she kept noticing that students would complain about problems with team assignments. Many university courses assign students to work on projects in groups, sometimes because the projects required more work than could be accomplished by individuals, and sometimes because the projects required access to expensive equipment that couldn't be made available to everyone separately. When Mary Lynn divided students into teams for a project, the next thing she knew she'd be hearing about how they were fighting or that one student was slacking or that someone insisted on doing everything themselves. Problems with teamwork and collaboration could outpace, or even swamp, challenges with the work itself. Students would bring the issue up in class, in office hours, and in conversation with teaching assistants, and they would write negative reviews in end-of-semester course surveys. No one was helping them with this problem.

Mary Lynn is one of those professors who is especially attuned to noticing how students experience the work that's assigned to them. She's an engineering professor, MIT educated, with no professional background in the issues around managing team dynamics, but she dove headfirst into learning what might be known about the subject of teaching people how to work in teams. It turned out that there is a lot of research, and research-based practical advice, available on the subject. (Search on "effective team dynamics" [ETD] if you'd like to know more.) Over several years, Mary Lynn developed an expertise in ETD and made her own contributions to the field, adapting techniques to use in universities and developing training methods. Her work made a demonstrable difference; people who learned her approach are simply better at working together.

The way Mary Lynn saw it, if you tell students to work in teams and provide no training, they will more often than not have bad experiences. They will fight, complain, and also not achieve the sort of learning outcomes that faculty aim for.

Looking around the university, she saw that the problem was widespread. A lot of classes required some kinds of teamwork, and in nearly all, teams failed to work well together all too often. Here was a serious problem, very common, and she had an effective solution. In just a few hours, she could teach students techniques that could resolve a large portion of the issues. It was a classic case of a real problem with a real product that could solve it.

But over the next few years, Mary Lynn became increasingly frustrated. She tried to get students interested in letting her show them how to work in teams effectively. She would say to them, "Don't you sometimes fight with teammates? Why don't you come and learn how to work better in a team?" While they would readily agree that their teaming experiences could be problematic, they were indifferent to doing anything about it. She felt the same kind of frustration Jim Balkcom did with Humminbird and Akmann Van-Mary felt with truckers. They all thought there should be more demand for what they were offering, but making the product better and explaining to the potential customers why they should use the product were not spurring demand.

This was Mary Lynn's situation when we first met her. Joining a cohort at the Center for Deliberate Innovation (CDI),

Mary Lynn, with several of her ETD-trained assistants, began a process that led to her doing hundreds of DPIs with students, professors, and administrators. Sure enough, at the beginning she saw nothing but indifference. She would lay out how she saw the students' situations. She'd notice speech acts (which are a kind of behavior) such as "We had a slacker we had to deal with" or "I ended up doing all the work myself" or "We complained to the professor and he said, 'You'll have to work in teams in the real world, so just figure it out.'" They would agree that this was how it often was. But that would be the end of it. Students didn't come for training. She also spoke to professors. They told her, "There isn't time for adding more material to the syllabus" or "They are going to have to deal with this sort of thing when they get jobs, so they should learn to deal with it" or "It's not my job to teach them how to work in teams. It's my job to teach them about [materials science/mechanics/physics/whatever]." Almost everyone could agree that there were markers (such as fights and poor outcomes) that indicated problems. Yet she could not get a sense of anything other than indifference from the interactions she was having. People readily talked about the problem, but no one seemed drawn to a solution.

Understanding problems from the customer's perspective is crucial but not sufficient. The way people talk about their problems doesn't describe their problems, exactly; it describes how they conceptualize their problems. Their words reflect—and are part of—how they cope with their problems. The difference is sometimes subtle. But it's crucially important because the discerning the difference between how a person sees their own situation and how it can be seen from outside can open a window onto authentic demand.

Keeping that distinction in mind can be difficult. At first when Mary Lynn heard the complaint that "we had a slacker we had to deal with," she immediately adopted this view of the situation as her own, and started thinking about how student teams can do a better job of dealing with slackers. But in office hours with Merrick, he asked her where the word "slacker" had come from. The answer was that in her hundreds of DPIs, students had frequently used the word. Merrick asked if there was any such thing as a slacker.

Mary Lynn looked into it, and it turned out that there was no such thing. The students getting labeled as slackers were victims of fundamental attribution bias. Students doing the work in a team noticed that some team members were not doing the work and attributed it to a made-up personal characteristic—they were slacking because they were slackers. But students who were labeled slackers turned out to have after-school jobs or children or language problems. The culprit wasn't a personality trait but a situation. That insight became part of Mary Lynn's ETD program.

Working with CDI, she slowly came to see the students' situations more clearly. As Akmann had experienced with the shippers and lumpers on the loading dock, the students seemed indifferent to the offering. That did not (necessarily) mean that learning ETD wasn't valuable to them; but as she explored the issue it seemed to lead her into a dead end, to get her stuck. It became clear that the students she spoke with were in one of two situations: either they weren't currently working in a dysfunctional team or they were. If they weren't, well, there's lots of research into "hyperbolic discounting," the very common error people make by discounting or ignoring the possibility of something bad happening later (the reason insurance is so hard to sell).

If they *were* currently struggling with team dysfunctions, they were too focused on coping with current problems to be attracted to training or preparation. They were looking for solutions, not for training in how to find solutions. Think of approaching someone in the middle of a fight with a coupon for karate lessons, or someone in the middle of a marital spat with a recommendation for a good family therapist. You wouldn't be met by indifference, but you would be met with indifference to what you are offering.

This indifference to taking up her offer of ETD training was a real roadblock. She was stuck. Once it became clear to Mary Lynn that she couldn't overcome it by finding the right "customers" or by coming up with a better pitch, she was able to take a step back and begin to think of the situation more holistically. She became interested in how the situation was perpetuating itself. She was confident that her ultimate goal was reachable; new learning objectives and new training and class offerings are adopted at universities, so ETD could be too. She just couldn't see how that would happen in the situations she was encountering.

So she began to look at the existing situation more closely. Perhaps the fact that students didn't seem drawn to learning ETD didn't matter! She started to wonder, "How do our students normally come to learn what they're expected to learn things around here?" The answer was obvious: students more or less comply with learning things that are course requirements, whether or not they're drawn to the subject. They learn because it's an element of their situations as students to study and learn what's on the syllabus. The path to helping students become more effective team members could be to get ETD into the course requirements. The results of ETD training—effective work within teams—were being demanded, so the training was implicitly a course requirement. It just wasn't something the professors were teaching.

This insight led her to shift her focus from students to professors. In retrospect, this seems like an obvious move, but it wasn't for Mary Lynn. In her mind, professors weren't part of the solution; they were part of the problem. She'd been lavishing her attention on the students and their situations, and paying insufficient attention to the professors.

So Mary Lynn revisited previously recorded DPIs with faculty members. She'd asked them, "Do your students ever have problems with teamwork and collaboration?" Of course they did. Nearly everyone she talked to had stories to tell about it. She'd expected this answer. "OK, so what do you do about it?" The common answer she got to this question was something like "I tell them that in the real world you'll have to collaborate, so they need to work it out." At this point, which came up in many conversations over months, Mary Lynn would feel an almost overwhelming urge to make a sales pitch. She wanted to say some polite version of "Well, you idiot, you could teach them this and this and this. Or why don't you just invite me to your class and let me teach it for you!"

She did make sales pitches a few times. It was hard not to. But she always got some sort of indifference in response. As she became more effective with the DPIs, she tried to notice how she might not be noticing something. She remembered the mantra "Know your customers better than they knew themselves." But what does that mean, exactly? How do you do it? In this case, she decided, it meant wondering how it was that professors were taking it on themselves to teach some things and at the same time not taking it on themselves to teach other things. That was clearly happening—but how was it happening?

Mary Lynn started speaking with professors to understand whether and under what conditions they taught things that weren't strictly on the syllabus. She heard about professors patiently teaching students how to use unfamiliar equipment. She heard about them helping students through calculations they should have learned how to make in previous courses, and about professors spending extra time giving students creative ways to look at a knotty problem. At one point a professor ended an anecdote like that saying, "I don't want them to think I don't care about them."

The word "care" hadn't come up before. Certainly Mary Lynn hadn't said it. She took note of it and decided to explore.

In her next conversations, she listened for words like "care" and "caring." She heard them more and more often. Caring about their students or being seen by the students as a caring professors seemed to matter. The way Mary Lynn was talking about her work on team dynamics began to predictably provoke professors into voicing worries about students thinking they didn't care.

Mary Lynn's first weeks of conducting DPIs were mostly focused on attending to students. She also conducted DPIs with administrators, but didn't notice, or wasn't able to provoke, nonindifference. She went down other paths (such as gamifying her methods to make them more attractive) that didn't seem to lead anywhere. The next six weeks were more about attending to professors. Finally, Mary Lynn was developing an understanding of the situation and how she could become a part of it.

The DPIs were open-ended conversations where she said as little as possible and did her best to avoid leading people in any direction. She had tried to pitch her expertise before, without success. But with this new understanding, she was ready to try another pitch. It went like this: "Do you know that when you tell students to just go figure it out because they will need to in the real world, they think you are saying you don't care about them? Give me two hours in one of your classes, and I can help with that." The responses to that were anything but indifferent.

Getting to that simple, obvious-sounding pitch took about three months, hundreds of DPIs, careful listening, and some difficult rethinking. On paper it doesn't seem like much. But the shift in behavior was electric. One professor responded by taking out his schedule and asking how soon she could come to his class. Others must have talked about it far and wide, because she started getting unsolicited calls to come and teach ETD. Before long, Mary Lynn and the people she had trained were overwhelmed with demand. Demand for her team training services spread from the undergrad engineering department to other departments, to staff teams, to the graduate schools, and then beyond to other universities. It has continued to this day.

CHAPTER 12
Your Deep Gladness and the World's Deep Hunger

We started this book by paraphrasing Frederick Buechner: "being an innovator means being called to where your deep gladness and the world's deep hunger meet." Throughout the book, we've made an argument that innovators get stuck, and innovation fails more often than it should, because innovators pay too much attention to their deep gladness and not enough to the world's deep hunger.

We've observed that in case after case. From Humminbird Fish Finder, where the gladness of making a more effective fish finder obscured the hunger for some weekend recreation. From GMR, where the gladness of building a revolutionary new technology to increase areal density in hard drives hid the deep hunger for greater reliability. From Mary Lynn, whose gladness in figuring out how to get students to collaborate more effectively hid the deep hunger professors had to be seen as caring for their students.

We've also seen how uncovering these hidden "hungers" (authentic demands) can lead to innovation success. From the simple inspiration of turning shame on its head—a hunger for pride—in Kibera, to the complex machinations needed to align not nots that launched WebSphere to become an $8 billion business.

We've unpacked some of how all this hiding takes place—the biases, cognitive illusions, and conceptual umwelts that lead to overlooking or not noticing or dismissing authentic demands that are hiding in plain sight. What could be more obvious than that recreational fishermen are drawn to recreation? Or that people taking spinning classes are drawn to engaging spinning classes? But it's hard to see the picture from inside the frame. Finally, we've described aspects of a culture and details of a tool kit that innovators can use to see into their blind spots to find the deep hunger that they can nourish with their deep gladness, and connect the circuit of innovation.

One of the things that hid in plain sight for Matt was the importance of unconditional positive regard. When Merrick first explained the idea, Matt thought "How lovely. Sure, why not paste that onto the culture we're building at Flashpoint." It seemed like a nice, inoffensive notion that didn't have anything directly to do with the work of innovation. Later, it became clear that holding colleagues in unconditional positive regard was a necessary part of the work. Because people couldn't see into their own blind spots, they needed help. And for that, they needed a culture of radical candor. But radical candor without unconditional positive regard leads to a culture of guardedness and fear—the opposite of what's needed.

That made sense. But it took longer to realize why unconditional positive regard is absolutely central to the work of innovation. The colleague stuff is important, but what's crucial is applying it to the customers. If you've got some invention in mind and you get it out in front of people, one of two things will be the case: they'll be either indifferent to it or not. If they're really indifferent to it, then you're sunk. For example, if they're actually OK with catching as many fish as they're already catching, then they'll be indifferent to any device, no matter how ingenious, that helps them catch more fish. But if they're nonindifferent, if there's an authentic demand, then you can be sure that on some level they're already coping with it. That's where unconditional positive regard comes in. Part of treating potential customers and clients that way is accepting that they are already experts in their own lives, skillfully coping with their situations. If their coping is inadequate in some way, that's almost certainly because the job of coping with something else is restraining them. Once you take the leap into treating them with unconditional positive regard, you open yourself to noticing how they actually are coping, and to all the things they're coping with. Innovations don't succeed just by solving problems. They succeed by solving problems in a way that also solves the problem of why customers haven't already solved the problem themselves.

Strikingly, as we've interviewed people who have been involved with Deliberate Innovation, we've heard more about how it has affected their personal lives than about its impact on their work as innovators. When you respect others as people skillfully coping with their own lives, you notice that you your-self live within an umwelt and a set of situations that might be different from those of the people you're with. When you notice others succumbing to biases out of common mistakes like fundamental attribution or confirmation bias, you can start seeing these same universal human failings in yourself, leading to more tolerance and more common ground. And when you start seeing how people's behavior is tied to their situations, opportunities to change things for the better start appearing.

We heard more "businessy" things too. One CEO told us that Deliberate Innovation took a lot of the alchemy out of innovation, made it more a matter of careful thought and less a matter of luck. One venture capitalist told us that he invested in Flashpoint companies because we produced better, clearer-thinking CEOs. Another said that veterans of the Flashpoint program could skip a round of funding, because they made their way more directly to becoming successful businesses.

But some said that unconditional positive regard was the biggest takeaway. We hope that's true for a lot of people. We called this book *The Heart of Innovation* not only because the four of us have spent a lot of our careers trying to get to the heart of innovation but also because of our belief that innovation has a heart. When innovators identify the gaps between who people feel they are and what they're committed to, on the one hand, and the options that are available to them, on the other, then they enable people to be more whole. Making that happen, through treating colleagues and stakeholders and customers with unconditional positive regard, is a worthwhile goal.

Deliberate Innovation doesn't promise successful innovation every time, any more than coaching promises that every race will be won. But from the vantage point of decades of succeeding and failing at innovation ourselves, managing innovators, investing in them, and mentoring them, it seems to us that we can all do a hell of a lot better. A world where innovators and their colleagues have a compass to use, where they have techniques to practice and get better at, where there are actually competent innovators, and where competence can be distinguished from luck, would be a world with a lot less waste and a lot more successful innovation, to the benefit of us all.

APPENDIX

DPIs Step by Step

This appendix is adapted from an unpublished workbook developed by the participants at the Center for Deliberate Innovation at Georgia Tech.

The DPI process has several steps, but it's not programmatic in the sense of following a script or checking off answers to specific questions. Several points in the process require creativity, courage, sensitivity, empathy, or other human qualities that can't be specified in a script.

Table A.1 is an overview of the steps of the DPI process, along with some particular risks and considerations.

Table A.1. Overview of the DPI process

Step	Considerations
1. Select an area where you have some experience.	Without domain expertise, you will miss important things and mistakenly consider trivial ones as important. Expertise generally comes from working in the business area for at least several years, on either the selling or the technology side.
2. Find people in the domain with whom to conduct DPIs.	A typical DPI process will take two to three months and several DPIs per day in order to reach reliable innovations. Founding teams build up to twenty or more DPIs per week. Finding the right people to interact with can be easier or harder depending on the domain. (It's easier to talk to consumers in a mall than vice presidents in Fortune 500 companies.) Often, setting up a process for finding and scheduling DPIs requires a lot of creativity. But because DPIs are largely conducted with potential customers, devising ways to find them and get their attention is crucial not only for the DPI process but for the future business.
3. Start noticing phenomena related to how the situation gets constructed.	The trick here is to pay attention to actual behaviors and circumstances, and not to focus on motivations or outcomes. It's very easy to get this wrong and to see a behavior through the lens of a motivation or outcome. Focus solely on what's happening, not why people are making that happen. The good news is that you can start nearly anywhere, with any phenomenon you notice.
4. When you notice a phenomenon, test for stability or invariance.	You do this by devising experiments to create obstacles, in order to see whether people act to overcome the obstacles or simply divert to other concerns. For example, if someone buys budget products, see if they'll stop buying when the price goes up. If they don't stop, then price must not be a stable consideration that you can use to predict whether they'll buy. Thinking of and devising appropriate tests can require considerable creativity.

Table A.1. Overview of the DPI process *(continued)*

Step	Considerations
5. When you find stable phenomena, work forward, backward, or sideways to build out your picture of the person's situation.	Working forward means paying attention to what would not happen in the future if the phenomenon didn't happen now. Working backward means looking into what must have occurred previously in order for the stable current behavior to occur now. Working sideways means paying attention to other people who are integral to the situation and starting to build out how it looks from their vantage point.
6. Pay attention to equipment.	In parallel with building a reliable picture of the situation, pay particular attention to the tools or equipment people use in the course of maintaining the stable phenomenon. What role do the tools play? What could be problematic about how the tools play their roles? Tools can be physical objects, but can also be names for things, skills that have been developed, habits that have been formed, and the like. Tools and equipment are described more fully in chapter 10.
7. Imagine new equipment.	On the basis of understanding the foregoing, imagine new tools that would be less problematic. Ideally, the features of a new tool are molded exactly from the situation.
8. Introduce new equipment.	Proxies for new equipment can be as simple as a few words that signal a unique understanding of the situation to the people in it. They can also include some kinds of minimum viable products (MVPs).

Exploring situations involves inductive reasoning, going from the data or phenomena to generalizations rather than the other way around. But the trick is to hold off on generalizing as long as possible. Instead, the job is to notice and piece together the phenomena without reference to anything general.

How to Prepare for the DPI

First, if you are doing a DPI about a topic or an idea and there isn't a person at the center of your interest, you are not ready.

Second, avoid showing up to the DPI and then after it is done asking yourself what just happened. Instead, you should show up with an expectation of what situation the other person will be in and then figure out whether you were right or wrong based on the information you find. Before starting a DPI, register some information and make some predictions about what you are expecting. Otherwise you will be vulnerable to hindsight bias. Registering prior views is a form of Odysseus bargain (see chapter 9). Knowing that they're likely to be led off course by a cognitive error, DPIers take steps such as registering their prior views.

Third, write down the following information before conducting the DPI to guard against hindsight bias.

1. Determine whom you expect to interview at the DPI.

   This should be the person you care about. Carefully describe the person in terms of their situations but without using generic categories. We often make the mistake of thinking of human beings in terms of properties, such as age, gender, race, height, or weight. Instead, think of people in terms of their situations or experiences. For example: "This person is a procurement manager. I expect them to have a list of vendor qualifications that they consult when considering a new vendor, and I expect them to be nonindifferent to the items on that list."

2. Describe the situation in which you expect to find the person.

Ideally your description should include the situation that the person finds themself in—for example, they are not just "a student" but "a student who has just lost their financial aid." The situation they are in is something that they're coping with. You would like to discover what they are not indifferent to in that situation, what is not OK for them.

3. What are they doing or not doing?

If appropriate, work through a situation diagram before the DPI to identify that person's equipment and connections. This can help identify some mechanical items and behaviors (things they are doing or not doing) that can then help you understand their situation and how they are skillfully coping.

4. List the evidence you expect to find.

You should be extremely intentional about what you want to get out of the meeting. In order for your innovation to become part of this person's situation, there must be something problematic with how they're presently coping in that situation. How do you expect that problem to manifest?

5. Plan a test.

What are you planning to say or do to elicit the evidence you're looking for? It is more useful to hear responses that disprove your hypothesis. Positive examples can create a false sense of confidence that you are right, and feed confirmation bias. Be careful to avoid questions that only yield positive answers (e.g. "Would you like to save money?"). It's frequently useful to think in terms of negatives here. So instead of asking someone whether they care about X, figure out a test or scenario that does without X and observe whether their reactions show indifference.

How to Show Up at the DPI

Don't show up in a superior or controlling position. For example, showing up as an expert researcher saying, "I'm going to do research on you," creates a situation that makes productive conversation difficult. Instead, show up in a one-down position. Taking the one-down position means you indicate that without their help you are in danger of wasting time and resources. This is an authentic position to take—by doing DPIs you are effectively admitting that you have not yet found a way to be meaningful in their situation. By taking the position of need and calling on another for assistance, you can be curious and genuinely interested in your customer.

Whenever possible, bring two people to a DPI: one to interact and the other to observe.

Once you have determined the type of person and situation you care about, find a way to identify them randomly. If you select only people you already know, you are more likely to introduce biases. Ideally the process for finding a person should be clear, but the person identified should not be known in advance. For example, if you are doing DPIs with faculty members, just walk into a building and go counterclockwise until you reach an open door with a faculty member inside.

Prompts to Use in a DPI

Decide on a prompt. The first sequence of DPIs is relatively free-form. You are not proposing solutions yet, so avoid selling or attempting to influence the person in any way. Your goal is to find some sort of relationship or transaction that you as an innovator and they as potential customers will be nonindifferent to. Keep in mind that in doing DPIs, you are acknowledging to yourself that you are not (yet) at that point.

You need to go into a DPI with a strong opinion loosely held. The strong opinion amounts to a clear sense of exactly what you're considering as a candidate for something to which the person will be nonindifferent (e.g. that they are seen to care about their students). However, in the likely event that you come across indifference to your opinion, your opinion should be loosely held so you can let go of it. Ideally you will say something that isn't in the form of a question, so as to avoid introducing demand characteristics (defined in the next paragraph). It might look something like "We noticed that . . . and we think that this is important, but then again, we may be wrong and it may not be" or "Before we spend more time digging into this, we wanted to talk to people like yourself who are in that situation." Full stop. Don't be afraid of allowing an extended silence. The person is often waiting to be asked a question, and they may take a minute to realize it's their turn to talk.

The term *demand characteristics* refers to the phenomenon where interviewees form an interpretation of the interviewer's purpose and unconsciously change their behavior to fit that interpretation in order to get a "favorable" evaluation. Although it is nearly impossible to prevent demand characteristics from showing up in the DPI process, it's possible to phrase your questions in a way that the demand is simply to get an answer, rather than to yield a particular answer. Here are three strategies for avoiding demand characteristics:

1. **Seeking the "no."** "We thought this would be something meaningful to work on, but after several conversations we don't think so anymore." Here, if the

customer is nonindifferent, they could exhibit that by saying something like, "No, you should work on this. Let me tell you why."

2. **Ask the same thing in a bunch of different ways.** Try different prompts and broach the same topic in different ways to ensure that any evidence of nonindifference is indeed valid.

3. **Have someone with no skin in the game conduct the DPI for you.** Sometimes, just the way you show up and present yourself can provoke demand characteristics. One way to test the validity of a nonindifference is to have another person who has no direct relationship to the outcome of the DPIs conduct the DPI. Because they have no skin in the game, they have no direct expected outcome to which the interviewee can orient and fit their behavior.

During the DPI

Before starting, begin to record the interaction. Ask permission, of course, but this is an important step. The D in DPI is for "documented." You can frequently provide the (not untrue!) excuse that you are not a good note-taker, and you want to be able to go back over the conversation to pay attention to the words that were chosen, because words matter. Also, it will keep the record pure, whereas your notes are more likely to introduce your own biases and your own words and interpretations of what was said. Video recordings are best, audio second best. If necessary, have a note-taker with you. If all else fails, take bullet-point or reminder-type notes during the meeting and write them out in greater detail immediately afterward.

The following are some things to notice and behaviors to be aware of during the DPI:

- If the person brings up something you didn't bring up, that's something to observe. You might say, "I noticed that I asked about A, but you brought up B. Can you tell me a little bit more about that?"

- Sometimes, it can sound as though the person is suggesting features or coming up with a product for you. When this happens, avoid continuing a discussion of possible features. You can say, "That is interesting. What did I say or do that made you say that?"

- Spend as much time listening and as little time talking as possible.

- Leave open space for the person to offer something up rather than simply have a transactional response.

- Try to listen reflectively. Repeat back to the person the words they use. This helps them notice things that they would not be able to notice themselves. "In your last response, you used the words ——; can you expand on that?"

- Avoid asking "Why?" Preferences and reasons will lead the person into telling a coherent story, which will introduce consistency biases that don't necessarily reflect the person's reality.

- Notice fundamental attribution errors, namely, when the response characterizes the person instead describing the situation that they're in.

- Be wary of stories that start to make sense; that might be a clue that you are hearing fiction. Reality doesn't sound like a short coherent story. It is OK to interrupt the person to end this natural tendency to introduce coherent stories.

- Keep the person focused on their firsthand experiences and not on things they believe that other people have experienced.

- Focus on the person's behavior. Can you get them to say things that they are doing or not doing while in that situation? If appropriate, ask what they would worry about if they changed or got rid of a particular behavior.

- Listen for nonindifference and make an effort to discern indifference. Is there something that the person is responding to that looks like something that they cannot "not do?" In other words, is there a behavior or speech act that they appear unwilling to not do (e.g. a shipper mentioning getting a good night's sleep)? If that's the case, then that's a place to dig further.

- If they make a little joke about something that seems important and then change the subject, this may indicate a coping mechanism.

- When the time comes, begin to close your notebook and signal that the conversation is over. Then, as you are leaving, ask if there's anything else they would like to share. This trick creates a sense of urgency, which is more persuasive than simply asking that question before you get ready to leave.

After the DPI

Review the recording with colleagues.

- Identify a few key items that the person shared.

- Keep track of time stamps showing when things were said.

- Did you notice what appeared to be a nonindifference? Why do you think that was the case?

- In reviewing the DPI, it's incredibly useful for you and colleagues to remind each other to slow down, focus on the phenomena, and avoid drawing conclusions.

Otherwise you will end up telling each other a coherent story instead of paying attention to the observations.

- Pay attention to what you said or did during the DPI. Notice your own biases and ways you may have influenced the outcome that may not have been obvious in the moment.

- Compare what the person said to what your expectations were of what they were going to say (written down before the DPI). This can often surprise you because the person might not say what you expect them to. Update your expectations for the next DPI.

- Develop a system for storing and retrieving the DPI recordings and your notes. Very often, people will hear something in the fiftieth DPI and realize that they heard something similar in the second or third DPI, but hadn't noticed it.

- Review the process of obtaining the DPI. Can it be improved or streamlined?

Sustaining a DPI Cycle and Bringing It to a Close

DPIs can be arduous and emotionally draining. To even begin conducting them, innovators usually must overcome a curse-of-knowledge misconception that DPIs aren't necessary, that they already understand the market and the demand. Even starting with an open mind at first, an innovator can find it difficult to notice a distinction between indifference and nonindifference. Ryan Jones, CEO of Florence Healthcare, one of the most successful Flashpoint companies, said that it wasn't until his twentieth DPI that he actually witnessed an emotional response to an authentic demand, and came to see a value in continuing.

As practitioners learn the approach, they typically build up to approximately twenty DPIs per week. The key to increasing volume is to continually assess and improve the process of identifying people to speak to and the scheduling process. One advantage of DPIs over some other types of customer research is that DPIs can often be very short, taking no more than fifteen minutes each.

Very commonly a cycle of DPIs will go through phases. During a ramp-up period, both scheduling and conducting well-structured DPIs are difficult, so innovators get sparse, low-quality data. Scheduling and conducting DPIs both improve through practice, and the cycle becomes a roller coaster ride. An innovator will see an emotional reaction that looks like authentic demand, believe they're on to something, and pursue it, but then further DPIs turn out to be contradictory or uninspiring—the potential customers are indifferent after all. In the middle of that low point, the innovator will see something else to pursue, leading to another encouraging reaction, one that might be genuine this time or might send them off on another wild goose chase. The cycle repeats until the innovator gives up or until they find something they can't invalidate and can build around.

NOTES

Introduction

1. Frederick Buechner, https://www.frederickbuechner.com/
quote-of-the-day/2021/7/18/vocation#. Accessed March
21, 2023.

Chapter 1

1. Clip from *The Dick Cavett Show*, aired September 4,
1970, available on YouTube, https://www.youtube.com/
watch?v=qFt0cP-klQI. Accessed March 21, 2023.

Chapter 2

1. Based on the authors' discussions with venture capitalists at
several leading firms, and experience with scores of startups.
2. "Top Reasons Startups Fail," CB Insights, https://www.
cbinsights.com/research/report/startup-failure-rea-
sons-top/. Accessed March 21, 2023.
3. Theodore Levitt, *Marketing Myopia* (Boston: Harvard
Business School Publishing, 2008). The famous line doesn't
actually appear in Levitt's book, though the idea does in
multiple forms. Levitt was said to have used it in his classes.
4. The authors have worked directly with Jim Balkom since
2011. Descriptions of dialogue are mainly paraphrased from
memory with Balkom's permission.

Chapter 3

1. The story in this chapter combines multiple conversations with Kennedy Odede and personal experiences in Kibera. It is used with Odede's permission.

Chapter 4

1. Archived at https://books.google.com/books?id=g5vMbM OTEE8C&pg=PA28&lpg=PA28&dq=byte+magazine+the +story+so+far+patterson+raid&source=bl&ots=hTKSjfOsT 5&sig=ACfU3U19s5Zlf_FZdL7UH1t4O3bD2bsT8w&hl =en&sa=X&ved=2ahUKEwiU6pz4zNT-AhWVElkFHQf kBhoQ6AF6BAgmEAM#v=onepage&q=byte%20 magazine%20the%20story%20so%20far%20patterson%20 raid&f=false. Last accessed May 12, 2023.
2. Frank Hayes, "The Story So Far," reprinted in *Computerworld*, November 17, 2003. Archived at https://books. google.com/books?id=g5vMbMOTEE8C&pg=PA28&lp- g=PA28&dq=byte+magazine+the+story+so+far+pat- terson+raid&source=bl&ots=hTKSjfOsT5&sig=AC- fU3U19s5Zlf_FZdL7UH1t4O3bD2bsT8w&hl=en&sa=X- &ved=2ahUKEwiU6pz4zNT-AhWVElkFHQfkBho- Q6AF6BAgmEAM#v=onepage&q=byte%20magazine%20 the%20story%20so%20far%20patterson%20raid&f=false. Last accessed May 12, 2023.
3. Arthur Schopenhauer, *Essays and Aphorisms*, trans. R. J. Hollingdale (London: Penguin Books, 1970), 41.

Chapter 5

1. William Ouchi, Theory Z: *How American Business Can Meet the Japanese Challenge* (New York: Avon Books, 1982).

Chapter 6

1. Steve Blank, *Four Steps to the Epiphany: Successful Strategies for Products That Win* (K&S Ranch, 2013).
2. Story and quotes used with permission of Elizabeth Cutler.

Chapter 8

1. Adapted from Daniel Kahneman, *Thinking, Fast and Slow* (New York: Farrar, Straus, and Giroux, 2011), 82.
2. John M. Darley and C. Daniel Batson, "From Jerusalem to Jericho: A Study of Situational and Dispositional Variables in Helping Behavior," *Journal of Personality and Social Psychology* 27, no. 1 (1973): 100–108.
3. The most comprehensive general discussion of the issue of dispositional versus situational behavior is found in Lee Ross and Richard E. Nisbett, *The Person and the Situation: Perspectives of Social Psychology* (London: Pinter & Martin, 2011).
4. Raymond S. Nickerson, "Confirmation Bias: A Ubiquitous Phenomenon in Many Guises," *Review of General Psychology* 2, no. 2 (1998): 175–220.

Chapter 9

1. Kim Scott, *Radical Candor: Be a Kick-Ass Boss without Losing Your Humanity* (New York: St. Martin's Press, 2017).

Chapter 10

1. Alexander Osterwalder, "The Business Model Ontology: A Proposition in a Design Science Approach" (PhD diss., Université de Lausanne, École des hautes études commerciales, 2004).
2. Research Gate abstract of Alexander Osterwalder's PhD dissertation, https://www.researchgate.net/publication/33681401_The_Business_Model_Ontology_-_A_Proposition_in_a_Design_Science_Approach. Accessed March 26, 2023.
3. Created by Business Model Foundry AG, Copyright 2020—Strategyzer AG, Zone Industrielle (ZI) Le Tresi 9B 1028 Préverenges, Switzerland, licensed under the creative Commons Attribution-Share Alike 3.0 Unported License, https://upload.wikimedia.org/wikipedia/commons/1/10/Business_Model_ Canvas.png, modified by the authors to remove graphics and text under category headers. Material

available under Public License at https://commons.wikimedia
.org/wiki/File:Business_Model_Canvass_template.png.
4. Story and quotes used with permission of Akmann
    Van-Mary.

Chapter 11
1. Story and quotes used with permission of Mary Lynn Realff.

ACKNOWLEDGMENTS

We acknowledge the people who have graciously allowed us to use stories from their lives and experiences in this book: Jane Achieng, Jim Balkcom, Elizabeth Cutler, Kennedy Odede, Mary Lynn Realff, and Akmann Van-Mary. We also acknowledge the people who have read versions of the book and spent many hours with the manuscript, providing valuable feedback, wise advice, and emotional support: James Altucher, Kendra Armer, David Chanoff, Eric Gold, Pam Gordon, Susan Hopp, Neal Malliet, Michael Massiello, and Mike Schatz. Lew Lefton and Nammi Verdire, fellows at the Center for Deliberate Innovation at Georgia Tech, produced a handbook on conducting DPIs that was the invaluable basis for the appendix. They led the way in showing us that the nuanced work involved could be codified in print.

Danny acknowledges Steve Mills, mentor and friend, whose brilliant intuitive insights and deep knowledge of IBM customers and clients allowed us to drive and build a $25+ billion software business. He also thanks John Swainson, Donald Ferguson,

Robert Leblanc, and Helene Armitage, who were invaluable colleagues in the very early days of WebSphere and helped shoulder all the skepticism and pushback that any transformation will meet.

Mark acknowledges mentors and colleagues Abe Peled, Ralph Gomory, and Brent Hailpern, who were instrumental in shaping his participation and understanding of the research division's role in IBM through a process called the Ten Year Outlook. It became the key to understanding why invention is not necessarily innovation.

Merrick and Matt acknowledge the colleagues, mentors, and friends who have taught them about innovation and joined them in the projects and experiences that have led to this book: Ravi Bellamkonda, Roberta Berry, Tal Cohen, James Coleman, Richard Dale, Dan Droz, Andy Fleming, Zvi Galil, Jim Gauer, Berny Gray, Jim Grosch, Heath Hyneman, Charles Isbell, Ryan Jones, Chuck Kaplan, Elli Kaplan, Annie Lai, Jeffrey Leavitt, Rhonda Lowry, John Mandile, Marc Morgenstern, Sig Mosely, Wendy Newstetter, Ron Nash, Orgesi Pandeli, Beth Polish, Chandler Powell, Toby Rubin, Mike Schatz, Bev Seay, Chrissy Spencer, Meade Sutterfield, and Kevin Wozniak. These people, along with literally thousands of other entrepreneurs, students, and workshop participants, have helped make this book what it is.

Needless to say, all mistakes and misunderstandings are our own.

INDEX

Note: Page numbers in *italics* indicate figures and tables.

ABOUT THE AUTHORS

MATT CHANOFF is a San Francisco-based angel investor and cofounder with Merrick Furst of the startup studio Flashpoint. He has served on the boards of early-stage logistics and cybersecurity companies, and currently sits on seven nonprofit boards in the areas of poverty, media, and education. Prior to his investment career, Matt was a management consultant in the electronics manufacturing industry, and served as chief economist for Technology Forecasters Inc. Previously, he directed the Asia program for the National Endowment for Democracy, and was a speechwriter for Senator Paul Simon of Illinois. He has a master of arts degree in international economics and politics from Johns Hopkins School of Advanced International Studies.

MERRICK FURST is a Distinguished Professor and the director of the Center for Deliberate Innovation at Georgia Tech (CDI). In 2011, he founded Flashpoint, a first-of-its-kind deliberate innovation studio, to develop formative leaders and exceptional technology startups. Flashpoint was the thirty-sixth startup accelerator worldwide, very early in the development of business accelerators. Merrick has been teaching entrepreneurship in an innovative form since 2006. He was the president of the International Computer Science Institute at UC Berkeley, and before that was a professor and dean at Carnegie Mellon. At Flashpoint and at CDI, Merrick works with hundreds of founders and innovators, and is developing the discipline of Deliberate Innovation.

DANIEL SABBAH, PhD, was the CTO and general manager, Next Generation Platform, at IBM until his retirement at the end of 2015. He was responsible for creating IBM's cloud platform and aligning IBM's direction for cloud and mobility. His career at IBM spanned forty years as a researcher and developer, and finally in IBM's Software Group as a CTO and general manager of various divisions. His innovative leadership helped pioneer IBM into open source in the early 2000s, well before it was popular. He was also instrumental in IBM's successful drive into internet software (WebSphere). Sabbah received his MA and PhD in computer science from the University of Rochester in 1981, where he specialized in artificial intelligence and computer vision. Sabbah was named a Distinguished Alumnus of the university in 2019. He also has a degree from the Wharton School at the University of Pennsylvania. Sabbah is currently a member of the Arts, Sciences, and Engineering National Council and the Hajim Dean's Advisory Committee at the University of Rochester.

MARK WEGMAN is an IBM, ACM, and IEEE fellow, a member of the National Academy of Engineering, and a Distinguished Alumnus from UC Berkeley. He has published and patented more than one hundred works, with more than seventeen thousand citations, primarily in algorithms, information theory, and software engineering. Among his works are ideas that are used in every web browser and every optimizing compiler. He was also a member of the board of directors for Biospecifics Technologies, where he helped grow its value twentyfold before it was sold. His work at IBM included participating in the ten-year outlook, through which IBM attempted and largely succeeded at forecasting where the industry would be in a decade. That work grew into his interest in understanding which innovations would succeed.

More information about this book and the authors can be found at Heartofinnovationbook.com. More information about Deliberate Innovation in general can be found at cdi.gatech.edu. More information about the authors' investment and company development activities can be found at axuastudio.com.

Dear reader,

Thank you for picking up this book and welcome to the worldwide BK community! You're joining a special group of people who have come together to create positive change in their lives, organizations, and communities.

What's BK all about?

Our mission is to connect people and ideas to create a world that works for all.

Why? Our communities, organizations, and lives get bogged down by old paradigms of self-interest, exclusion, hierarchy, and privilege. But we believe that can change. That's why we seek the leading experts on these challenges—and share their actionable ideas with you.

A welcome gift

To help you get started, we'd like to offer you a **free copy** of one of our bestselling ebooks:

www.bkconnection.com/welcome

When you claim your **free ebook**, you'll also be subscribed to our blog.

Our freshest insights

Access the best new tools and ideas for leaders at all levels on our blog at ideas.bkconnection.com.

Sincerely,

Your friends at Berrett-Koehler

Certified

Corporation